The Ungrateful Child

The Ungrateful Child

The Child Within - The Memory Remains

JOHNSON MAJOR

PARTRIDGE

A Penguin Random House Company

To order additional copies of this book, contact
Toll Free 800 101 2657 (Singapore)
Toll Free 1 800 81 7340 (Malaysia)
orders.singapore@partridgepublishing.com

www.partridgepublishing.com/singapore

Contents

Chapter 1   The Beginning of Life.................................9

Chapter 2   It All Began Here...................................12

Chapter 3   Lessons and Message, Understanding 15

Chapter 4   Accident feeling in fault.........................20

Chapter 5   Pressured and Punished 24

Chapter 6   The Little Kind hearted Thief 32

Chapter 7   Being in Fault, even when not...................36

Chapter 8   Toll taken effect.....................................40

Chapter 9   Seeking Logic and happiness...................46

Chapter 10   Two years of School Happiness 54

Chapter 11   Ending Appreciation with unawareness
             of what's to come 62

Chapter 12   Introducing my humiliation...................66

Chapter 13   Incident with Understanding, and Warning..........73

Chapter 14   Standing my Voice.................................85

Chapter 15   My Prerogative, my only resort to Freedom.......... 101

'Life', in open Air, begins in '1978', Gravity at its fullest, playing its 'role', as we are still 'Living' the 'Great Journey to the Unknown'. . . The Land of the Giant, 'Though, the Land of the Free', I was 'Born', *"UNGRATEFULLY"*.....

CHAPTER 1

The Beginning of Life

Shrieking Cries, heard travelling through the 'Hospital Ward', the sound of a 'New Born'. First Breath of Air, 'Meaning', its first experience, being Competitive, slightly Stubborn, and all that needs is, Adjustment to new Surroundings. Although, unseen, it is the 'Exchange' to 'Oxygen', Also being it's first time, with 'Unawareness'-most would say it, a 'Healthy start'.

'Behind the Doors'- for those who heard cries, not long later, would have heard a distressed male's voice, calling for 'Help', as moments later, 'Nurses rushing into the Labour Room', followed by the Doctor.. Meanwhile, as the Child had been taken for Cleansing, by a Nurse following Procedures;

Second check to make sure, that the Lady who had given 'Birth' was at Clear, was at fail to do so.

See, at Labour, the Newly Born was attempting a Daring Feet first Entrance, to this Magnificent World of Mystery, Not so good of an idea, and was pushed back inside with plans to turn the Baby around, to Enter the Zone, 'Head first'.. As it seems, somewhere along the Line, the Umbilical cord had been pulled with enough force, to only wound the Ladies 'Womb' heavily, then left untreated from unawareness.

The Doctor who had rushed into the Labour room, guided by the Husbands hand pointing, to what was a large quantity of Blood under the bed his wife lay, and still losing Blood the lady was, with the base of her bed leaking blood at fast pace, whilst the colour of her skin changing rapidly - within an instance, without 'Hesitation', the Doctor called out to the Nurse, requesting a Long Needle, which he then Dabbed into the lady, who was Stone cold with Purple Blue splotches, as if looking at a Dead Corpse that had been gone long time before.. Everyone who was in that Room was surely at certain, not to ever forget that Moment, as explained to me, the moment the needle had entered the flesh, was that moment life had been restored, as the cold looking skin, transformed, to a warm glow with rosy red healthy appearance, and with no delays the doctor had ordered refill Blood to save the lady from dying,

Both Lady and child were granted life further more to the future, to an unexpected thrilling experience; One thing this New born child was not aware of, 'Was' the Future ahead for 'The', would be hard, costly, and irritably Faulting-even if not at fault, 'The' was to be the 'Blame' or be 'Punished' every step of the way, for 'Everything' or 'Anything' that had ever gone wrong..

This is the view of remembrance to a life I lived, and was forced to live, although some thought, this would not leave trails of long life Heartache and future disorientation, - for 'The, Only,' ever wanted to live a 'Normal life'...

Problems in Families occur all over the World, with children growing up amongst other classmates, adapt to an understanding, comparing the differences between each individuals lifestyles, realising that not everybody is the same, learning many families are of difference to methods, that are made from different experiences, cultures and so-on, from happiness to sadness, 'Proud' with a feeling of 'Purity', or 'Shame' as though to be guilty of 'Sins' not in fault for, feeling safe, or afraid, the children are the future, and the past creation had given Mankind the opportunity to experience, the best of what could have been, a 'World of Unity', for all Nations to group as one, who would lend their peace of mind, which would teach, preach, and show act of togetherness, with patience, 'Love', 'Respect', 'Courage' to 'Dignify' one another's 'Presence', with details to why we are here on Earth without questioning needed - for the answer is simple - 'LIFE ITSELF', means 'LOVE', to all who are still here present, living a breeze, or struggling through it, either way, we have been granted this 'Opportunity' to make something of it., its never too late, but 'Dreadful' to some, who feel they had given their best, to prove their well intended nature to their surroundings, to only be looked down at, as if 'The' were mocking the crowd, or hadn't the faintest to what 'The' was on about, though be aware, this saying sticks forever - 'WHAT GOES AROUND, COMES AROUND'-, and surely the time had 'Come', and although in ways 'The' hadn't been patient all through; 'Time' had always been 'There', 'Steady' and 'Patient', which had given 'The' enough 'of', to figure it out – 'TIME'! Time is of the essence, though, 'Time', will always be of Presence - the time has come for 'The', to give his all-

-This 'The', is 'Me' - the Child who had grown, to 'Forget' any 'Resent'-

Born a loser, as 'Quoted' by specifics, but me, with 'Ambitions' to 'Succeed', and I wont stop until I pass the finish line, because I am the only person living in my body, in 'Flesh', the only who really understands myself, with 'No Right' to anyone to misguide me, as I will be my own carer 24/7-365

CHAPTER 2

It All Began Here

Dad had spotted Mum on a Ship Destined to Australia on a 37 day Trip, along with many other Foreigners, who had fled their Country to make a better life for themselves; 'Their excuse'..!

As the Ship had Parked, with No Hesitation, Dad had followed Mum for three days, persuading her into Marriage, somehow he managed to do so.. I know its not right to Assume, (as Assumptions are often, 'The Mother of all Failing Points), though it makes perfect sense - Arriving to a country of the unknown, feeling alone, the only thing that reassures you of warmth, and security, also the fact both speaking the same language, is the voice of a man insuring a life of 'togetherness', and mum had agreed to dads proposal, so they got 'Married'!

First is my elder sister, 'Mariah', followed by my brother, 'Thomas', then I'm Next, and 5th, classified as 4th, is my little sister, 'Joanna' - in between Joanna and I, was my little sister, who had passed away not long after birth., we didn't speak of her, not to upset mother, as, remembering on one occasion the conversation was at air - my sisters arteries had clogged, which disallowed oxygen to the respiratory system. Mum had gone through a 'Psychological stage', 'Unstable', soon after to make up for the loss, had given birth to 'Joanna'. So the matter had been kept 'Hushed' for safety reasons, concerning matters towards Psychological upset.

I well remember my first frightening experience was at the age of, 3,1/2 at approximate, when mother decided on this particular day, to go shopping with a friend. I suppose this friend she had met, was by the same kindergarten mum had sent my elder brother to. I could also say understandably, that mum was a little furious and fed up with me - I could be a hand full, majority of the times, and she in need of an hours break, – deciding to leave me with my brother, with approval by the kindergarten teacher on duty until mum returned; well, i guess mum hadn't expected me to throw a tantrum which explained Attachment, this embarrassed mother as it seems, me on the other side of the fence rails, force squeezing my face through, screaming for mum, feeling as if she was giving me away forever;

I could not escape from this jail type building, with no allowance on my exiting, Tall Barred Gates being solid., - as it was the first time to part from mum; so mum swiftly turns around and shouts, **'Shut up'**, your embarrassing me, but 'No', I continued on frantically, with mum replying, **'You Ungrateful child'**.

Having children at three and half of age should have been tough for many parents, who had on their own nurtured without help by others, as it being the stages where the child, had learnt through the basics on the wrongs and rights, with the childs ability to decide for itself on many accounts, such as the dont's and do's, deciding on the activities prefered with desire, let alone the stages of walking, and running, playing with toys freely, without help needed, minds full of adventure etc.. I was still wearing nappies at this age, because, i still remember like it had been yesterday, as my father had me on the end of my sisters bed, he changing my nappies, with he moaning at me, forcing phsycology down my throat, he saying, '**Hurry up, get out of your Nappies, your a 3 1/2 year old donkey, and your embarrasing me infront of your mother**', he made me cry, and fear each time he had attended to my needs, without realising, what i feared more, had been the way of apprehension on dealing with us children, especially at these times, though in fear of their mentality. (I could never recall good happy feelings when being taught).

Many people that i have come across who i have asked relating to their child hood life, can't often remember events when at very young age; though, noticing many people who answered 'yes', were those who suffered deeply, with flashbacks, and memories implanted within, a scar to remind them, to never forget, whilst noticing, that the majority who came from a good natured/nurtured home, were to be less creative, slightly jealous, or little dull, or frightened of us who they knew, we had pain inflicted upon us. Maybe it made us look reckless towards others, they understanding we came from disasterous climates, presuming we'd become followers, some people felt sympothy, even if they found us fun, though, depending on the severity and difference of abuse, higher chances we being risk takers, adventurous, careless or disorientated, caused from past, or maybe just neither, and some of us were just of gentleman type, with respect, as to treat people with opposite conditions, as how our parents did to us.. that was me, the gentle man towards strangers; it was so much easier to make someone happy, (the, who were out of my circle), i felt appreciated, they made me feel worthy of my being of presence, in a way that allowed Sanity to guide me towards rashional decisions, teaching me more of the decent values of Life, more in that way, that 'I could never achieve at home' with my own members methods of dicipline.. (abusive and careless, un-experienced with selfish, and stubborn grudges, only bossing me around, for self image, lazy beneficials).

CHAPTER 3

Lessons and Message, Understanding

Later on, it was my time to start Pre-school, learning after a couple times, mum would soon return picking me up afterwards., pre-school became fun, because the activities the teachers had planned were, new and exciting, and i as a child in my house, hadn't the right to express my 'Inner growing passions towards hobbies', (as to allow a child to grow with talents and show creativity), maybe the reason was, I thought mischief, which seemed 'too out of line' for mum to allow me, at my age to express my interests, always applying the 'No', without ever explaining why. 'Could I have known at this age'?, where-is, in my mind, viewing a pathway to creation, with hobbies allowing me to participate or interact with my inner desires and curious appetite, to new experiences? 'Suddenly out of know where', **'Smack'**, I was struck on the side of my head, I hadn't realised at the time, but this was my Mothers hand, slapping me ever so hard, compression slap to my 'Ear', which at the time of impact, creating a Popping sound, leaving me in major shock, with a constant ringing tone in the 'Ear drum', and 'I', in a dumb founded pause, - hadn't been expecting this, as I can't recall what bad thing I had done, to deserve without warning, a **'Concussion to Remember'**!.

Still in pre-school, I can remember occasional visits from **Dad**, he would come to see me, if he had finished early, or on a split shift basis. He was working for the **Government**, *'The Met'*, which was for a Tram service. He was the provider of the **family**, and the only means of income, food, shelter etc. Mum (with no other option), stayed home with my little **sister**, 'Joanna', 'Newly born'; when dad entered the *kindergarten*, he would first speak to the teacher's, explaining mother's situation, though always leaving his flaws out of the equasion; he was always good at talking 'for others', especially when they hadn't been present.! He then would approach me, with sorry eyes, looking innocent and helpless, as if feeling sorry for me too. We would sit together, beside the sand pit, and he would carve into the Bark with his pocket knife; by the time he had ended his talk with me, the Bark had been transformed into a boat, as the sand pit on this day was filled with water. For that moment, he made me *Smile,*- for him, this was a **relief**, he knowing the situation at home was *tense! (though overlooking the fact, he had hands in contributing to my anxiety)*, Mum was going through a rough time, my brother an Epileptic, 'me', nearly *killing mum at labour*, also the fact she had lost a child, she found it difficult to juggle problems after problems.

Going back to my brothers situation, whilst at four (4) of age, was feverish with the 'Measles', mum failed to admit him to hospital care on time, as dad had mentioned to me. I suppose both were thinking, well, this is just a 'Minor' and passing illness, seeing after five (5) days, his temperature rising heavily, with no allowance of control, Believing with her methods she could heel the matter!, Eventualy his condition could not be eased, so Mum decided 'Professional Advice' was at must at all costs to be seeked, even though she didn't like it when people other than herself, opinionated upon our families concerns of our well being, feeling as if threatened by misguidance, or to correct her methods, she felt *implications against her, so to be in denial with stubbornness, otherwise, you were in for a hefty ordeal with lectures, such as with a thorough example (**"I am their Mother, i know what's best for them, it's not your business"**). Meanwhile, attending the **Hospital,** Thomas was pushed through to '**First aid**', as the doctors realised the severity of the situation - Examinations began. The doctor had injected medication into my brother, with then, a prescription to good rest, keeping a close eye on him, Thomas was sent 'Home' to recover.*

The following day, as explained, my brother was found in bed, with his eyes faced to the left, and his body in a tensed posture, though shaking frantically with froth spilling from his mouth; 'Something was seriously wrong', so mum and dad being very worried, immediately rushed him back to Hospital.

Thomas had been examined by the doctor, and sadly diagnosed with 'Brain damage' and an 'Epileptic'. He had been deprived of immediate treatment, with then after, the doctor's application of medicine; Thomas's body hadn't the strength to cope with the late dose applied. To my knowledge of common sense, seeking attention should have been 'thought' sooner.

Now, don't get me wrong if i sound my voice with a tone of revenge, or if it seems i want to inflict pain against my family, as that's the last thing i would want, (but this is 'My Life', and i say it like it was, is and what i'm dealing with), 'Really', do/did any of these three members take in consideration, the pain i still hold from the Scars left behind, and as i am well aware of it this moment on, two members who damaged my future, are still fighting for wrong causes, selfishly and faulsly, against me to keep their so called 'Innocense' from proving them guilty. - "SHAME ON YOU BOTH", they had both used my mother, and she still isn't aware of it, and 'if she is', pride won't let the shame show(which keeps her closed in suffocating mode). It would kill her to actually see into the matter, and find by psychology it's Surprisingly true, this goes for all the Mislead People, because once you have lied and escaped with it so many times, for something serious, having planned with a cunning way to look Truthful, also playing with the weaker minded, you can fool many, and are liable to live the rest of your life 'Fooling Yourself, Fooling Others'..

My Mother used to warn me all the time, not to follow my fathers footsteps, and i must have thought she was just 'Mean'., heck, 'SHE WAS RIGHT', although she was wrong with methods, using 'Psychological' and 'Physical Pressure'..,

I Forgive her, and Apologize for being the 'Ungratefull Child', though do believe, she should have been looking more at my sister, as she new or should have known Mariah was 'Jealous', and 'Evil', after we were born.., Mariah became very Protective of her territory, never to share her property with us, and played very rough with me as a baby, when mother would leave me with her.- 'i know this, because, one of her class friends who broke up friendship with her, had found me wandering the yard at school and approached me, then complimented me on how strong i must be, to be living with my sister, as she being Mariahs ex friend, could not cope with Mariah. **"She's Too 'Bitchy', thinking to High and Mighty of herself, being a Tattle tale, 'Always' wanting and seeking Attention".** These were the words spoken to me, as she had me around the tennis court walls, boosting my confidence, though mentioning to me how Mariah had grabbed me on one occasion, when i had been crying as an infant slapping me and shaking me frantically, then bouncing me off my bouncy chair with a thud noise on the lounge room floor, because i hadn't stopped crying which made her crazy, and Mariah broadcasting the event laughing Satanically. Though their was no one there important to her, who could report the incident, just my brother, as i can imagine she manipulating him well, and he with disability.

Which brings to my attention, how many parents leave their babies, with children who seem mature, though, when they turn their backs, 'The things that go on', without mentioning.

Message: **"Parent's.., whatever you do, Don't leave your children with your other children alone for one second if you have trouble with them, if you really love them, and seek the best outcome towards their future and yours!, PLEASE, keep and open mind, always expect the unexpected, Especially from your first born child if having children after those".**

I Understand my Mother Now, 'More than ever', she held me inside protecting me for those 9 months, she dressed me and fed me, raised me, and if the father wasn't there, she'd be the father at his absence, a Mother is more to Love than a father, especially if your father was good at making children, but hardly ever being home, leaving all the resposibilities to mum, as he would supposidly be at work, but more to evade us to attend his pleasures, as i soon found out by myself with time showing the way., but what could i do, he is my father, so i naturally shut up.

'YOU CAN CHOOSE YOUR FRIENDS, BUT YOU CAN'T CHOOSE YOUR FAMILY'. I never had favored that saying, until i actually felt the same way. You see, things don't always stay the same.

I Truelly Love my Family, without the Abuse, though, i guess we can't all have Paris...

CHAPTER 4

Accident feeling in fault

I remember Easter very clearly at pre-school, because from this day, I can still remember the ringing sounds of a bell, as the teachers had put our tasks to an immediate halt, as we were called in from the playground, to find 'Foot prints' the size of 'Bigfoot', all over our classroom floor. All children amazed, following the foot prints, to only be lead through a Wild Goose chase, we were allowed that moment of curiosity, then the teachers quickly gathered all of us children together, as to focus our attention towards a fairytale story; when all of a sudden, as loud and surprisingly new, all of us children startled, we faced towards the entrance of our room, to where the ringing sound came from, we all paused with a posture in suspense, for at least half a minute, expecting something, or anything to come round the corridor corner, but nothing!, then all of a sudden, just on that moment ready to turn back, with a look of confusion, the 'Easter Bunny', big, pink, with white ears appeared, he began to hop round our room, i remembering the long whiskers, and chocolate eggs being given out to all of us. This was a day we'd never forget, as our minds were jilted with, 'Fear', though within an instance, 'Relief' to see that the bunny looked friendly. All was over within 10 minutes; The fairytale of the 'Easter bunny' was then read to all the class, explaining Easter.

On one evening, as mum had returned for me, we had approached the pedestrian traffic lights with Diana, a classmate; I remember her long brown wavy hair, down to her waste, hazel eyes, with a gorgeous face. Each day we would walk the same path. On this particular day, mum had been occupied with conversations, she with Diana's mum, and us kids had raced for the pedestrian crossing switch, I hearing mother with a raised voice, **"Children, wait"**, though as children, in our minds, we felt, because we had seen the green walk sign, with allowance to cross, the cars at a complete stop, we dashed for it; as Diana took off before me, she had made it to the other side safely; I approached the end, when out of nowhere, I had been struck by a large car, as it had accelerated suddenly at high force, remembering its colour being 'Beige',(Ford XT, an old Taxi) it had taken me at least, 25 metres along the road, also remembering the driver beeping the horn in my ears, as I was hoisted on the front end, then tossed into the middle of the road, where their was a nature strip dividing, ongoing, oncoming vehicles. Mum was shocked, she screaming at the top of her lungs frantically, and I had wet my pants, crying, I could not walk, remembering the ambulance arriving, I had been placed into the vehicle. By this time my father had arrived to the scene, and I could hear the voice of the driver explaining to my parents, that only one of them could take the trip to the hospital with me. Mum had given me a blasting at with her screams, as if I had done something wrong, naturally, I was afraid, i answered to the driver, I wanted my father to take the ride with me, but dad had mentioned to me, he having his car with him, he would meet me at the hospital, so mum jumped in, sitting opposite me, with a greasy, disgusted, and worried look directly staring me to shame, punishment had commenced without delay, and words had been spoken from her eyes, informing to me of consequences yet to be placed.

later we arrived to the Hospital 'First Aid' entrance, the nurse wheeled me off to the ex-ray room, from there, to the examination room, to find the reason I hadn't the ability to walk, was from 'Shock'; I remember as the doctor had his hammer type instrument(Reflex finder Knee Knocker), as he had gently wacked it under the knee cap, my knee jolted, and with his deep voice, he said to me, **"Wipe those tears son, your a strong lad, you will be fine, no broken bones, your a very lucky boy".**,(i don't know if i was in shock from the accident itself, though i was definately frightened of the price to pay, with heavy consequences awaiting me, on my return home) then I was released, and sent home to rest. In a way, i felt more comfortable at the hospital, and more afraid to leave, as i feared, with visions that things would get rough at home.

Their was a long silence on this drive home, with it being at least 45 minutes from the Royal Childrens Hospital. Once we arrived in the gates, my dad made a small test to see if i could walk, though i made it difficult, so he picked me up, and carried me to my bedroom, placed me on my bed, then he had left the room, and no more than half a minute, i could hear mother, blasting my father, on how she wants him to - **"Do something about him,**(me), **he's nothing but disobedient",** blaming dad of how he only ever teaches us everything, and anything other than educational and productive... i had fallen asleep, spent the remainder of the day in bed, next day, I was running again mischief. From that day on, mum was ever so strict, like a 'Prisoner' under constant 'Surveillance', and if suspected of any wrong doings, even if it hadn't been the case, I would cop a hand full of 'Physical or Psychological abuse', she thinking this was the 'Right kind of Methods' to discipline me, as dad had been absent many hours of the day, always mentioning to me of when she was younger, **"Your grandfather, made me wash his clothes, wash and cook, polish his shoes, at the age of seven, and even if i was good or bad, i would cop the belt, because i was the eldest in my family, and my sisters and brother cut my dresses in my closet"**. She would always compare her lessons of life to me, making sure to put me in place, without realising, this was destroying me, and it always ever seemed, that i was the only ever getting this poor of an excuse treatment, with she then adding, **"I Nearly died for you at Birth, and i am your Mother, so, 'You Have to listen to me"** I was surely destined to doom, as every day felt like Hell.

CHAPTER 5

Pressured and Punished

It was now time for grade one (1), remembering at school 'Mariah and Thomas' had been attending; it was 500 metres close to our home, very convenient, at close range walking distance. Every morning walking to this school, Mariah would take over the role of mums and dads, making sure we'd keep on the footpath, forcing me and Thomas to walk at least 15 metres in front; I suppose this was in fear of embarrassment, as mum would dress my brother and I, with identical clothing, also the fact Thomas had his disability, with me being the 'Stupid Little Brat', as referred to, each and every day. Mariah loved her independence, as I was just a set back to her image, she adding **"You're an embarrassment, you little Dork"**.

As soon as we had entered the school grounds, Mariah had sent me off to class with orders, pointing her finger to the direction, with an angry face, **"You know where it is, "Now Go"**, she then turned her back and left.

One inparticular day in class, i disticly remember this moment, as my teacher should have been lectured, i believe it was cruel of her not to allow me at urgent need. (considering my age) as i had raised my hand, seeking permission in need of the toilet; I had been denied the allowance, as I was busting and couldn't hold much longer. The teacher had explained to me, class was nearly over, so you can hold on till then - but I couldn't, with no more than a minute passing, i let full toiletry go in my pants; this was an unpleasant moment as 5 seconds given maximum, all class students took a waft of dreadfulness, grabbing their noses, in pronto mode deserting the vicinity, with a perimeter of, well, how can I explain it - all backs on classroom wall, windows flung open, and within 30 seconds, all students hung their heads outside, with a loud commotion; I had been left in the middle of the classroom floor, face, blushed, with a guilty and worried look on me, as I realised my teacher then, pointing her hand towards the door, screaming, **"Out, Principals office, Now"**. Shamefully, I rose with fear, picturing a Dragon awaiting me, ready to punish me; I was too Scared to go, so the teacher had asked one of the students to accompany me to the head office, with a letter of explanation; I guess a letter was the best of choices, anyone next to me would grab their nose, cover their face with their sleave, or hide their face in their top, in fear to speak, encase this smell was contagious, looking at me as if wanting to curse at me; I felt ever so small, but the worst was yet to come! No more than one (1) minute, arriving around the corner, and I momentarily sighing with relief, a familiar face set my heart at ease, forgetting that this person was also furious with me, prior to, for whatever it was I had done that i wasn't aware of - 'yep' you guessed it, the Wicked Witch of my life, my hateful sister; boy, did she look pissed. First thing was first, she was very apologetic towards the school, for her brother who humiliated her in life, as she then grabbed my hand with force, violently pulling me, and i struggling to keep on my feet, as if a speed boat pulling a water skier out of control; she had done this all the way home, but, as exiting the school grounds, she had been mumbling to me that, **"When mum see's you, also hears**

why you were sent home, your going to cop it, 'you 'Ungrateful little brat', all you ever do is embarrass and ruin my reputation''; we had then arrived home, Mariah started to growl at me as we approached the front door, making sure to alert mother, no need to knock, the door had swung wide open to find my mother standing their, with her fists nudged against the side of her hips, with a cross face;.. This was one of those moments Mariah loved, as Mother didn't have the chance to open her Mouth to question the reason, for being home so early that day; Mariah had explained every little detail, though both mum and sister forgetting, or knowing, but not allowing me the chance to explain my side of the story, they hadn't asked me. As I tried to explain that the teacher hadn't let me go to the toilet, I copped a slap in my face, with mum growling at me too, **"You ungrateful child", - you should be ashamed of yourself, you have to embarrass me everywhere I go'!** Mum then hurried me to the bathroom, to disgustingly hate me, whilst washing me in a furious manor. By the time mum had finished, my Buttocks were covered with slap marks, remembering this very clearly, smacking my wet skin, as mum made sure i would not to do this to her again, as each time I was forced to sit down, I would feel pain.

Each day in this house was, Judgement day for me, the day would not end, if I didn't get punished.

It always happened during the time dad was absent from home, so he hadn't the faintest, to why I was miserable each and every day at home, but he would always put smiles on our faces, even if it meant to pose funny faces or say and do silly things, 'not a good idea', 'Actually', this was a Big mistake, if mother had found us laughing, after our moment of dicipline, She would get very hostile with dad, always directing the blame on him for the reason I was mischievous, (she had a Right) that he being the coach of all bad doings, 'Overlooking the fact that they blaming eachother, with physical and mental abuse placed on me, would only confuse and disorientate my thoughts and stability, also lowering my self esteem, without understanding that we are children, we need Guidance towards love and support, teaching of productive doings, not lessons of physical interaction towards direction, with brutal actions..

I guess my mother had approached this school many times that year, as it had only been six (6) months into, when remembering she was very upset on a particular day, but Surprisingly, I hadn't been the centre of attention on this matter; the school had refused my brother attending, as he had an 'Epileptic Seizer' on the premises, which frightened the other students, also he being different from others. - I figure the teachers were unsure with fear on how to deal with this disability, and cancelled his admittance, as he being a liability to the future of many around him; mum lost it, handling the matter unprofessionally.

The time had come to move to another School. 'St Peters', the next closest educational facility, roughly 300 metres more the walking distance, the school had accepted our attendance. Each day was more a struggle, allowing my sister more time to 'Psychologically Pressure' me on this longer walk. She was 'Grumpy', 'Mean', always explaining, how I was her 'Embarrassment', ruining her reputation, she then adding, **"Don't come near me at school, you Ungrateful Little Brat"**, naturally I would ask why, she would swiftly turn to me, grab me by the collar shake me in a manor, as if to say, wake up you fool, with her excuse as, **"Because, I don't want Spoilt Little Brats Destroying my Reputation, I have friends you know"**!, then out of nowhere Thomas with a raised voice says, **"Come on you guys, cut it out"**; we both froze, as this was very weird coming from my brother, he rarely ever involved himself in retaliating disputes, so naturally, we both shut up continuing our walk to school.

I being in grade one (1) continuing what was left of that semester, with the whole class seated, story books in front of us, when on the loud speaker our teachers name was called, requesting her to attend to the Principals office. During the time she had gone, one of the boys threw a scrunched up piece of paper, to 'Karla', on rebound, she had called him a name, then right after, she had been chased all over the classroom, she then had jumped on one of the tables, with attempt to leap to another, with miscalculations, she missed, colliding face first on the corner of the table, she slashed all side of her cheek very deep, all students panicked, with commotion in the class, next classroom door had swung open, with our classroom door next opening, to find a male teacher standing their. Karla had been rushed to the school nurse, then not long later the ambulance had arrived, we were not to see 'Karla' again at our school.

During that week, I don't know why, as I had been called into my teacher's office, I had noticed a bag of chocolate Easter eggs, as she had often excused herself from time to time, to then enter her office, and no more than 15 to 20 seconds she'd return in front of the black board again.

'This was my moment', as the loud speaker calling for her to attend the main office immediately; well, 'Guess what', i felt, since i don't get any of these sweets given to me at home, I found my chance to enter, successfully stealing one of her eggs; (yes, the depribed little thief) I quickly enjoyed gobbling it up, returning to my seat, trying to eliminate any evidence in the mouth, when she had returned to the classroom., 10 minutes had passed, she decided it was time to enter her office, leaving us for a moment, then my concience had kicked in, with my knees knocking, 'I' had panicked, as she came out looking deep into the eyes of all students, with a question I hoped she wouldn't ask, but there it was, **"Now, Who is the little devil that stole from my office"?**, suddenly, their was a long pause of silence.. nobody answered, she then warned everybody she would find out who and punish the culprit. She then called in one of the other teachers by telephone, and within 5 minutes both teachers came up with a solution, with all children one by one being forced to open their mouths, it was my turn, she then grabbed my t-shirt, from the right shoulder, dragging me to the side of the class, and asked me in front of the class room, **"Did you steal my easter egg and don't lie".,** i was paralysed, i hadn't the ability to speak, as she could see my eyes watering, she knew i was guilty, therefore, I had been busted, chocolate had been spotted stuck on the rear wisdom tooth, with me being sent to the back of the room, to stand on a chair with a 'Dunce' hat, looking like a 'Witch', though prior to this punishment, I was forced to put out my hands, then whacked with a 'Ruler', until tears came rolling down my face, with my teacher explaining to the class, thieves were not welcomed in this school, and the next person would cop it worse., she adding, **"This is a lesson to all, to remind you of what awaits the next person, who decides to do such a thing here".!**

It was time that my Mother found out about this crime, resulting in losing my lunchtime, as all children were out in the yard enjoying their break, i had been followed by my teacher all the way to the Principals office, to find my mother standing, with her knuckles nudged against her hips, greazing me off in massive disgust, though, her real thoughts were, 'of embarrassment', trying not to show it in front of the teachers and principal, as all eyes were on me, with all who had been in presence, (evaluating this family).., 'Boy, was i to cop another ordeal returning home', but who was to know exactly on the events that commenced in our house.., the look was obvious, as i had seen it a hundred times over, mums eyes spoke again, eye balling me, not to let me out of sight, to make sure that i knew it, that i 'was' destined to heavy Punishment, to last a lifetime.. I felt like the 'Filthy animal', ever so light headed, reality felt like a dizzy spell, flowing instantly from the brain, with the pressure releasing to my body, and my Heart had sunk with the weight, ever so heavy, i could not even think. I felt like i had left the planet, if anything could save me at that moment, it would have been forgiveness, and a guiding hand with a lesson of sofisticated methods, but, that was out of the question, it was deliberate to make me suffer.., i needed to sit down, i hadn't the strength to stand, my legs became Gello, and i reaching out for the chair, and my mother calling to me, **"Stand up you ungrateful child, you should be ashamed of your self, i feed you at home, how dare you"**, she added..

The truth of the matter was, in my house we were to eat 3 times a day, morning, lunch and dinner, though being forced to eat food, we dislike and 'If' we don't eat it, mum would cancel our eating allowance, meaning, no more for that night being sent to bed without. I'd be pelted with any hard object, rapidly, if i had been caught sneaking a snack, in between at times not ideal in mothers mind, or if i had mentioned i was hungry, i had been dissallowed, not just by mother, as most of the decisions, had been made by my elder sister, as she spoke english, and was my mums favorite, she would teach english to my mum, and with her 'Dominant', 'selfish', and 'jealous mind', would intervene, in order to make sure, no leanience came my way.., truely from the heart, she wanted all children members to suffer, as she had been the first child born, she was so upset with us for the attention focused our way, even though she received all the quality wants in life, such as, a dressing table, her closet, her own bed, allowed to play the radio, go to her so called friends, who would only teach my sister, how to use and abuse her own family, plus much more; and all i had was a toy car, a few toys, that were always taken from me, even a christmas or a birthday gift that i had received, and if relatives had given me any toys, mother disliked that idea, as she didn't fancy others giving gifts for no reason, as i hadn't deserved them; She had put them in a hiding place, on top of her white closets, that not even a Chair could get me up their, anyhow, i found creativity a specialty, finding many ways to Compensate the loss of wanted toys, by creating an inner mind, towards visual fantasy, such as forcing myself to daydream of thoughts i invented, in order to make my own cherished moments, that way i found happiness in a place, where 'Nobody' could invade, and destroy..

CHAPTER 6

The Little Kind hearted Thief

I had now moved up to grade two(2), with a little more understanding to school Rythum and dicipline, though, without perfection, not realising their would be other obstacles involved, such as having a Crush on a classmate. She had me in a Trance, as I could not help myself, I would sit in class as the teacher had all students seated on the floor, in front of the Blackboard - this was an easier method of grabbing hold of all students attention, meanwhile, I was sitting behind my future wife, as I visioned it would be this way, with my young at age puppy love, - I guess this was because the soothing flower scent, pouring from her surrounding held me in a Hypnotic stage, and the fact being, I had never dwelt, or had never met anyone with these aspects. I was sucked in with Uncontrollable desires by her presence, as I really needed her to acknowledge me, I would sit right behind her sniffing to where the scent came from. It came from her long, straight, shiny brown hair; - at first she disallowed me to do so, i was playfull and after doing this a few times, she didn't mind, she would wave her hair in my face, brushing against my nose. The feeling so much like an angel guarding me, as nothing bad could ever refrain me from living life as if it were a fantasy, come to reality. (i was in a goofy trance in love)

The following day I had attended class, and in my possession I held a 'Ring', ripe and ready to be handed over, to as it felt at that moment - the girl for my future. 'Puppy Love'

I don't know at the time, 'if', it was for Revenge, or with the Fact of how Jealous and Selfish she was, not allowing fairness towards the other children in the family; with all cost to destroy ones face to gain access to all she could call her own, as she felt, as once rubbed in my face on one ugly occasion, quoting **"I**(she) **was 'born' first, so I have more right to more"**, with a posture of High and Mighty, with **"as for you, you have no right to any matter, in fact you shouldn't be allowed to anything good"**! So, as for 'I', feeling 'numb' from all the abuse, I swiped the best Ring that I could find; knowing their were consequences. Love to Hate were of the feelings at the time, being as implanted in me, I hadn't known any better.

The night Before I had robbed from the Cold Hearted, with kindness to donate it to whom I Believed, 'Deserved it 'more'... 'The girl for my future'; well, I was young, I felt in Love, but with a little help, that was surely not going to Happen; as the owner of this Ring would definately, be looking for it soon after,; this was 'for sure'.! – I was 'Busted', fingers were pointed my direction, as I was the only one who fit into the Jigsaw puzzles, missing piece, 'easy pick', all odds were against me, I was heavily punished, 'Brutally scarred - (branded), like an Animal; my first lesson to why 'Love' can hurt, as she frantically, lost her anger, by pulling my hair, slapping me in the face, also can still feel that moment when, she had pushed and pulled me in a manner, as you would, when throwing an object to people in a circle - left, right, here, there, until that was over, i would get slapped and punished by mother, and with it being theft, i also copped an after shock by my father, as he would say to me 'Come

on Son, why do you put me to shame with your mother', this talk
placing me at fault, i felt ever so numb with guilt, as to beleive i had
been the real problem, i hadn't the answer nor feel the need to.. the
answers were obvious.! Meanwhile, this 'Ring' belonging to Mariah,
was a must at all cost, she regaining access to it, and she did, **"Over
my dead body"**, were her words, **"Will i let this go, and from here
onwards, you better watch your step, you little Creep, make sure
you keep well away from my property, Ungratefull little brat"**.

I had been Publicized in school, which allowed others to push
me around, through out my school career, as i recall one event that
baffled me, and until this day, i still don't understand.., it was one
difficult morning, being a normal day in, day out routine, from
the moment my eyes are opened, until the day ending, pushed
and pulled, verbal abuse, like a torture you wished would just give
you a break, in need of, a 'Swallow of Air', just a moment to gather
yourself, to give you the courage, and strength to continue on with
the fight, as now, i'm feeling Numb from all 'prior to', that i had
received. In the school yard i had been pushed around, and naturally
i didn't know what i should do with this bully, as he actually hurt
me, and i could not escape him, so i searched for Mariah around
the school building, finding her in the far end of the school yard.,
she swiftly turned on me abruptly 'Disowning, and Owning me'
in front of her friends, shouting at me, angrily turning me around,
'growling', **"Don't come on this side of the school again, your not
old enough to be here, nor welcome, keep away from me, you
little brat, i don't want anyone knowing you have anything to
do with me"..**

*With many of the other things, 'good' or 'bad' that I had done,
Mariah Classified this incident as a major Offence, with hate, she
'Horridly' despised me, then making sure that the future for I was
Ungratefully unpleasant, reminding me constantly how much of a mess*

up I was, and what a waste of space I am to the families Reputation.
'Unforgettable', though i don't blame her, as today, i can say that without
a grudge, even if she had scarred me in life deeply, i always find my
way through tough times, as i have full awareness of my Flaws - what
happens furthur more, will be the hands turning back time, placed upon
an hour where their will be a very long silence, to those who ever opposed
me, as i had been unarmed, defenceless, stadistically brutalized forced
and sentenced to be a Psychological wreck, without understanding their
methods of actions, would provoke matters into depth on a high rate
of consequences, and i want 'no' part in the returns, as i am a simple
man with the highest of expectations, with love to my surroundings,
free natured person, i like to see everybody having a good time, and
succeeding in life; as **"Everyone** *in* **'My world'** *is considered* **Equal***".*

CHAPTER 7

Being in Fault, even when not

Despite all the abuse through out all the years living at home, living in these Circumstances, i noticed children in my class's, were of similar or had encountered some abusive 'act outs' from their own family members, leading to, 'fathers' sent to 'Jail', either it being 'Drug' related, from 'Alcohol', 'Physical Abuse' or 'murder' associated crimes, ranging from a variety of reasons, 'Mothers' had abandoned their mother hood responsibilities, as they had given birth at very young age, not understanding how to deal with parenting, in fear of their parents or the boyfriend, not being ready, wanting abortions, she not wanting, resulting in seperation, and finally the children paying the price, and a list that goes on and on..

Even though school was a dread to attend, 'Most of the time', *(for the reason being, or it seemed to me, the other children being smarter than I, 'Realistically' this being untrue, it's how i felt, and in a way, how i was forced to believe, with all the suppression left on me to feel; Other classmates thoughts were at view towards goals near success, 'possitive and cleaner than mine'; My* **Mind** *was* **Constantly Throbbing with Pain,** Always disturbing me, *a continual after shock, of what took place at my home, would finish there, but,* **like a 'Shadow' follow me at all times, all places.,** *and if for a moment it were that i had*

*drifted into space, this would be 'My' World', with **visions** of how i*
wished/pictured life should be, in order to find happiness, and a place
of safety), i should think that it had kept me alive, being less at home,
if it may be, allowing mum to calm down, find her peace, and i being
apart with distance from 'Mariah', and also the hard handed father,
who whenever pressured to dicipline me, would have blown me with the
*heaviest of batterings, uncalled for.., 'for me', **Relief and free** 'from*
*'**physical or Verbal contact**', momentarily, i had been in an activity*
of enjoyment, like in the playground; Recess or Lunch, were mainly the
reasons i liked school, no one to boss me around. i chose where to walk,
what to do, also being that i hadn't enjoyed my self at home; and then,
***'Drats'**, the bell, i would Sigh, and back to class i'd walk, (i'm now*
*Contemplating in mind) the teacher may ask me a question, and **'What***
***if'** i don't know the answer, 'What if' i can't answer correctly, and if*
they would call my parents, again, i would feel Humiliation, though, it
never happened, i found this imparticular teacher, had common sense
in understanding each of our values in growth and development, Mrs
Whell in my mind was great with methods; even it being, she knowing
of my family history, she gave me leaniency, as i can only remember her
faintly, like on one occasion she had placed us all in 5 different groups,
to exercise our vision and Reflex skills, she actually laughed with me,
as i had been very sharp on this activity, she made me feel worthy of
being in that moment, though, now i write of it, i do wonder if she had
a mental vision of me being slapped, coming from behind me, from the
side of my face, allowing her images to reenact and discover the reason
of my ability, seeing objects coming from behind ears, gaining access to
*sharp and quick reflexes.. '**God Bless Her, where ever she may be**'*

Grade 3 went by, without my acknowledgement. maybe it being
that my teacher had no grudges, she was a humble person. I can't recall
any harsh moment in her class, perhaps it being that my sister Mariah,
hadn't been in the school any longer, she was now in high school, also

the fact of my little sister, now being there in life, as she being born last, meant responsibilities, as the abuse had been less from mother. Family members being preoccupied excessive on other areas, though, i had always been under surveillance, tabs were kept on me 24/7, by the happy to be informent of the house, 'Mariah', she never missing a moment to climb the ladder of payback, and setting me back, without reason needed, minute after minute; so, i find my way to happiness, Stored, all in the mind.

*I just knew i was not like other children ('normal'), i had another style of vision, put to an Halt, until one day Due to heal myself, i would brush my shirt off clean, to then realise, now it's **'My Time'**, until that break comes, my journey continues, and as they say, Go with the Flow, and only Time will tell..*

*These were my heaviest years, struggling with myself, with my surrounding, struggling with the fact that, the children were occupying their time with activities, that i had been dissalowed to do at home, activities that i would severely be punished for, like i said, 'i would be punished for, and be placed in fault, even if i hadn't been the cause, or blame to anything major'.., **"For Crying out Loud, give me a break"**, it was mind baffling for me, i felt like 'The Deprived one', this was 'Torture' living at my place; though at school, teachers Quoted these kind of activities, such as, playing ball, sports, running with the children, acting out our talents, with characters etc.. 'Educational for Mind Expansion', towards the young growing Minds; and if i had brought these lessons home from school, they were hazardous to my mental, and physical health.., 'Entirely, Not my fault', as this had been part of school Curriculum programs.. Also adding to the fact that this was 'Primary school', as some would say, not so important of a matter, the children are young, they have many more years to develop, they don't need the extra attention, or somewhere along those lines, in order to evade responsibility, Time and Effort. Others who know of* *wisdom, who are loyal, know that every little bit counts.., but those who simply, couldn't care less, or look the other way, either don't have the experience, or patience to acknowledge the severe faults that arise in the future; it doesn't matter, Blame the kids, because they never listen, but for the children who had parents, felt like orphans, when seeking attention, being pushed aside, with a reply, "**Not now**", or "**Be quiet i'm watching t.v**", again, along those lines.. in my point of view, every little bit does count, because, when looking for the root of the problem, you will always find the answer/solution, and one of the main reasons why children go sour, 'Are' the cause of 'Parents'.., family', unfortunately, their are many people who become parents, who can't facilitate their child with the correct foundations required, and many who can, 'but fail'.., many who love their children with their life, should do some research, if in need of the know, to a healthy family life, also it being both parents working together, as they vowed in church togetherness, with equality, til Eternity(death do us apart). It's simple, teach yourself, ask questions.., circumstances are not always met with a smooth comprimise, though don't get me wrong, situations are also not of the same nature, meanings are many, such as, their are always two sides to a story, or theirs more to a story than meets the Glory, with a way of discribing 'difference', to each individuals journey, that led to happiness, or sadness, to understanding, or not, or just don't have a care in the world, as they themselves hadn't a fair chance, passing their grief to the next generation, without understanding, until too late, we become damaged goods, uncooperative, to later fault us enough times, until, we then become 'The' Fault, "For Real".*

CHAPTER 8

Toll taken effect

Here i am now in grade four, not aware of my future situation, just on the verge to sinking further more, to stages of deppresive pressure, and i can't feel it's presence closing in on me, as i am still young and active, with the ability to heal now before the toll takes effect, though the people who say they Love Me, are not living up to their words, behind the scene, disrupting, corrupting my well being of 'Focus'.

(I Remember a time when i had been listening in on a conversation, at the age of fifteen, to how i had been focused, and smart towards educational equasions, or how i had been very sharp, lasting until grade four; then a Dramatic change Occured, with a sudden lack of concentration, with a detour steering me to disfunctional instability.)

I guess Mariah thought she owned me, as she played the role of Mum and Dads, when they were at rest(placing her in charge), as she had been the oldest, and favoured her for being educated in higher ranks. Dad would be at work, or most of the time, 'Supposedly',(though, i later found out, if he would finish early, he would dash over to my relatives, to be less at home, as anyone would feel ashamed to have us as a family, as our family being different, where ever happiness would be, or those who would laugh at his entertainment and sillyness, he'd prefer it there; and throughout the years of him doing this behind our backs, he spoke well for 'Us', 'Against', informing to the people how my mother didn't like to travel to relatives, for the reason being, dad would speak against the family, blabbing his mouth without a thought to himself, how this was the reason to the main problem. 'Mum was right'), 'I don't blame him either, he hadn't finished school, meaning he being uneducated, and hadn't thought anything through except, the easy way out, and always entertaining, though always injuring himself when at young age, and disobedient, bringing grief home (my Grandmother had informed to me on many accounts)!

As for Mum, she would sometimes head off to the shops always leaving Mariah in charge,(as getting all the children ready, or taking us with her, was a choir to dread, so it was easier to leave us at home)., Damn it, the coast was clear, i was an easy target to antagonize, and surely enough, the taumenting would begin, by ordering me around, and if i would dissobey her, she would verbally, and Satanically push me around, as i well remember, one occasion which made me cry, with me being called the sore loser, ending off with me pulling her hair after she punching, kicking, and drag me around whilst threatening to tell my mother, that i had caused a riot, always placing me in fault for her anger, as i hated ever so much she ordering me around, abusing me as her slave. She would make me play a cruel game, 'who could pull the front of their pants down then up the fastest', and of course, i would lose, being that i was the male, i would always get my organs in late, with her standing their pointing and laughing at me, and me crying, **"Well that's not fair"**, then she would crossly say, **"Tough luck you stupid little Brat, it serves you right"**. She would always make me her Slave, clean this, do that, get away from there, come here, go and get it **"Now before**

you Cop it, you embarassment to the family", anything but nice, and when mum would return, the pleasure was all hers, to inform to my mother, the very moment she would enter the door, she'd announce that i had started it all, then laugh behind my mothers back, over her shoulder, making sure i could see her, as mum would shout and smack me in the face, anywhere she could inflict pain on me.. I was never heard, never given a chance to explain, 'Nor to be Right', day in, day out.

(So, i don't expect anybody to have understood me, as all true colours acting their revenge behind doors, leaving no trace on the real picture; 'The' who hadn't known the severity of the situation at hand, towards the reason i had drifted away, with lack of concentration during school, in class? My Focus had been fully towards 'Freedom, and 'Anxiety'?, natural instincts, or at this age too innocent, trying ever so hard to be patient, though, ever so in need to grow 'Wings and just fly away to a place, where all had been given a fair chance, 'Peace and Tranquility',,, - 'My Imagination'.) -- 'My World'

Mark would have been my first friend in grade four, as he lived just around the corner from my house; though, friendship did not get off to a great start, as we both had our first brawl outside our class, during lunch break. I can't remember how it all began, he scratching at my face, instead of punches, snarling at me, and i followed by pulling his hair, then not a moment later, we were pulled apart by our teacher, then sent to the main office for our Verdict.

Although we were sent to be punished, we had enough time to apologize to eachother, on the short walk to the Principals office. The Principal realising we felt remorse towards our actions, so, decisions were made with leniancy, by letting this matter slide, not reporting it, as it was totally clear, their had been no need for another episode by my mother entering the school., as each attendance by mother, meant that all people in the premises, knew of her presence, with more phsycological disturbance placed upon me, and all those around, equalling to distractions. Although the school revolved around dicipline, with this wise action made, i am sure they felt a 'Time out' had been needed to all, as they too were feeling the pressure, indulging an unbearable peak into my life, and how i lived it 24/7/365; I know they wondered how i felt, and how strong i had been, dealing with it full time, where a short moment was too much for others to bare.

*Somebody was sure to give me credit for keeping Sane, and the definite of all, credit given by my own members of my family, was at the fattest of all chances, as they believe until today, that i was the blame for all wrongs in our Life, so i deserved the punishment received. I remind to you each and every day, when i had copped a hand full of abuse, my mothers excuse to why i should at all cost listen to her, '**Because, i nearly died for you at birth**',(The same excuse to suppress my feelings making sure to be in control) and with the times Mariah had been blasting me, on her occasional tantrums when she'd remember to rub it in, "**You Little Brat, you destroyed the family**", and if that wasn't enough, each afternoon, my father had been pressured and forced to smack/belt me, but on his own behalf, brutalize me with the heaviest of force as you would, when swinging a cricket bat., though, he'd play rough to show up to mother, then 5 minutes later as he would hear me still crying(I Could cry all day, as there had been nothing to smile for, remembering in rewind and forwarding the event. If caught happy i would cop it even more)., he would find me, away from mothers sight, then approach me and grab me tight, hug and whisper in my ears, "**I'm sorry son, i had to show your mother, i am doing my job as a father, and i want you to know, I 'Love You', you are my favorite Son**"!.. (i had heard him many times he thinking, we wern't listening,* *saying to my elder sister, that she was his favorite, then he would repeat it to my little sister, and also saying to my elder brother, that he was his most favorite son)* **'Yeah Right'**, *it's hard to believe him, after he had done that enough times, i felt Numb, and mixed up inside, asking myself, 'How could someone 'Love', whilst Brutally punish you with violent force, then tell you they Loved you., it must have been* **'Love to 'Hate'!**

Mark and i living close to each other, also going to school together, often found eachother across the street of my house, with me finding an opportunity, escaping to the park across our house. I managed to sneak out of the house, finding a way to enjoy the very little time i had, before mother found me missing from home. We had found an old car bonnett, then placed it on the foot path as a Ramp; Mark Rode his bike at full speed flying over the ramp successfully. He then allowed me a turn at it, as i did not own a bicycle. I did the same a couple of times, until i decided to charge towards the ramp at full speed. I flew over it, though this time i had lost control on the landing, and found myself in prickle bush on the nature strip, along side the foot path. Not a good outcome, as my whole body, mainly my buttocks were full of prickles, i painfully stood up, ooh, and ouch, mark started laughing. My mother witnessed the whole incident frantically calling out to me. Mark then panicked, being afraid of my mother, he picked up his bike and sped off home without looking back.. I being sore as ever followed my mothers screams worrying, and soon enough i had been in the lounge room, being shouted at, whilst my clothes had been savagly ripped off of me, "**Stand still**", she growled, "**And Quiet, it's your fault, that's what you get for not listening to your mother**", here we go again, i thought inside, as mother had been pulling and tweezing at the pricks. She at each prickle, would joilt my body wih shakes, and growl, mumbling at me, "**I hope you learn your lesson, as one day you will remember your mothers words**", and with my elder sister in the backround, "**Don't allow him out again, the little Brat**", as she was the coach of all unhappiness, planting thoughts in mothers head, poisoning the Leaniancy in all matters, to get her way 'Always'.

CHAPTER 9

Seeking Logic and happiness

I can't remember many moments being allowed out of the house, as once or twice, during my life at home, had i been granted the chance to retrieve the mail from the letter box, mum later realising that i would use that chance to admire the other children in the neighbourhood, playing ball, riding their bikes, or hide and seek, so naturally, i would reach the letter box, then quickly, sneak to the children, but it was a fail, no more than 10/15 seconds later, my mother would rush out to the front yard shouting, "**COME HOME NOW**", with her knuckles nudged aginst her waste, as all activities from the children would come to a shocking Halt, they then would evaluate for that moment, realising what was happening, and watch me walk, hunch backed, towards mother; as i would aproach i took my time doing so, and i could hear the children asking eachother, "**Why doesn't that lady let him play outside with us**"?, "**Poor Boy**", *('Yes', 'Why'?, i ask myself, as the more you dissalow, means the more we want to be free, and accidently be carelessly mischievous, let us grow Up, 'Educated', without the 'Bitterness'. But 'No', Only ever teaching us always of how the people are bad in this world. Atleast teach us the right from wrong, also how their are 'Good and Bad people', with explanations why, on each account, we are Sure* *to be fine in Life, We need Positive Guidence to Succeed, rather than digesting Grief, feeling leftout all the time, and surely untrained towards communicating socially with others).* I eventually reached my mother, she swiftly grabbed me by the ear, and directed me to the entrance of the house, she forced me inside, then she had turned back, walking towards the Mail box. I quickly ran to my bedroom to the curtain, i peered out my window, to find my mother on that exact moment, looking towards me as she had been standing next to the mail box, i quickly pulled back from the window hiding under the window seal, with no more than 10 seconds i heard the front door close. i got up off the floor, then glanced out the window towards the streets, and before you know it, my mother had been standing behind me; **"What are you doing"**?, in a loud startling voice, as i hadn't heard her approach, **"Get away from the window"**, as she then entered the room, and walked over to the curtain, and shut it completely, screaming at me, **"I don't want to see you again looking out the Window, now go to the lounge room where i can see you, you ungratefull little child".** So i Naturally paced myself that way, through her bedroom, she then shouting, **"Not through here, your not allowed this way, Go around"**, i turned back towards her, and tried to pass her quickly, copping a heavy hand on the back of my head. I almost collided with the door frame stumbling with the force of the smack, and mad a dash for the lounge room, sitting on the floor next to the curtain. I found my chance to peak through the curtain opening. Mum had been washing her hands, when Mariah had entered the room, i then jolted in fear, staring in her eyes, realising she greasing me off, staring back at me with an evil look. So i sat on the couch like an innocent little boy, with my hands together on my laps. I remained in one place until i felt i was in the clear. I waited a moment realising no one had been checking on me, so i quickly turned around towards the curtain, put my head through the two openings, watching all of the children having fun, wishing i was there with them, asking myself, why i was any different to them, then all of a sudden, out of nowhere, 'SMACK', i jumped in sudden pain, it was my mother with a wide wooden spoon. **"What did i tell you, not to look through the window, you are not missing anything"**, she mentioned in a furious tone, **"But why, all the other children are outside, why can't i have fun"**. I bravely asked. **"Shut up, don't talk back to your mother, I don't care what the other children are doing, their parents don't care for them, that's why they let them in the streets, now sit down away from the curtain, i'm not going to tell you again, and don't let me catch you, otherwise i'll tell your father"**. she replied. I had been so confused and said in anger, **"It's not fair, i never get to do anything, i hate it here"**. She then smacked me in the face, and pelted me some more with the spoon, and directed me with it towards the front door, though in the corner behind it, she made me stand on my Knees until she said when it was over, **"don't move from their or you'll be in big trouble"**. She turned her back on me, heading off towards the kitchen again, as soon as she had left the room, my elder sister entered, i looked around, to find her poking her tongue out at me, placing her hands on the side of her head, waving them at me with an ugly posture, mocking me, as to say 'ha ha, serves you right'. I could hear her confrontating with mother. Never towards helping the situation with family matters, though to benefit for her own well being, as she learned how to manipulate mother, with Psychological methods.

Mariah had selected **'Psychology of Arts'** studies, which meant, learning the mind of others, and the ability to make Sane look Insane, also make the Right into a Wrong, or vise vursa. Never the less, this was a profession of distruction mode, playing with minds of others.

Meanwhile, i was still on my knees, 45 minutes later, with my knees ever so numb and i tired, physically, mentally, i was exhausted. I had started drooping, my buttocks touching my heals, and every now and then, you would see either my Mother or Mariah, pop their heads round the corner to see if i had been at the corner on my knees. (None of the other children(brother or sisters) received this treatment, and i believe it was the reason, mum nearly died for me at Birth, and i seemed disobedient towards her, so with retaliation not able to control me, they naturally faulted me for Everything, even if i hadn't been in fault). "**Stand on your knees properly**", screams my mother, with another 5 minutes passing, i couldn't bare it anymore, with me sitting on my heals, again, "**I can see you**", mum roars. This was '**Mariahs**' doing, 'The Informant', making sure i would suffer.. The time came, where i could no longer stand on my knees any more, and this was it, my mother came from behind, and pulled my ear, and growled "**Stand properly**". "**But i can't, my knees are hurting me**" i cried, "**Good, next time you listen to me, this will teach you to disobey your mother again**". This treatment kept on, until my father returned home..

'The Keys', i then heard keys, what a relief, it was my father, i rose with the chance of feeling free, as the door opened, i would have been the first to greet him. "**Hello son, how are you**", he would ask, and i would hug him, without saying a word, and start sobbing, letting my self become jellow, as i had no strength left in me, i didn't let him put me down, as he tried to release me. I hadn't the muscle to stand, without my father knowing my condition, he let me down slowly, i was like jelly oozing down to a puddle, then here it was, time to comprimize the excuse, Mariah would quickly cut in, saying to me, in front of dad, though to manipulate his moment of analysis, as he suspected something was up, "**And don't think your in the clear yet, you little trouble making Brat**", then she would turn to dad, and say, **"You better do something about him, mum can't handle him anymore"**, he would ask **"Why"**, Then she explained the whole situation, as if i had committed a Sin of all sins, he would then turn to me and say with his hands open and apart, **"Why son, why when i'm not home you are always naughty, when i'm home, your a good boy, what's happening with you"**?. (exactly, I had always been a good boy, though when he had turned his back, the ladies of the house made an issue into a sorry selfish act) I looked down, to the floor in shame and disbelief, that he too turned on me, believing by word of mouth othes, though he was tired also and didn't punish me, though i felt punished enough, i felt 'No love', with my thoughts all spinning as i looked up to the ceiling, it had been spinning also, and i could not control it, not even if i closed my eyes, i would get a migrane, feeling very faint, ready to black out, and if that wasn't enough, my mum would come back to me, and shout, **"And who told you to move from the corner, get back there Now, i will tell you when your finished, You Hear Me"**. She could see at that moment i hadn't been well, so she turned her back, and went back to the kitchen. Relieving me momentarily of her guilt, and my punishment.

(Excuse me as i write this, i will now take a break, as walking down memory lane, Is too much to bare, my head throbs, with flashbacks to an uncalled for journey, feeling powerless, with my sister in control, she made it a mission to have me in a low class mode, for the rest of my Life), the 'Scars Remain', and i try ever so hard to pick up my life, without hurting my family(Wife and Daughter).

They are the reason Life has more to offer, God Bless them both.

Writing this, i am in my 30's, remembering all as if it was yesterday, now realising, many casualties of similar neglagence, take on their journey till the day they die, a bitter memory that has or had destroyed their most 'Sacred years' of their lives, and what i'd have to say to all the victims, Where is, knobody heard their Cries/Pain, as most likely they hold the dark story inside of them, in order not to destroy anyones well being, though allowing the guilty to walk free, walking over us, with the ability to destroy more people, this can't go on, 'let go', Our lifes are greater than those who pose for Materialistic, or Image purposes, those who are 'Greedy and selfish', 'the' who worry about what others think of them, and what if someone sees wrong in them, they would blame another, to cover up their humiliation, but to only expect the **'Spotlight'** *without sharing it, are of those who have the 'Mental Issue', in need of help, if they make belief to others, that others are something they arn't, and are of those, who 'Should be Punished Severely', and in my point of view, we so called troubled victims, are the more deserving and caring, if it had effected us to a suffocating point, where all we need, is a chance or break for it, to perform our talents, that we possess, are of the highest standards anybody had overlooked, as to them we seemed different, or Untrustworthy; This is truelly untrue, we are very Trustworthy, though to be feared, as they know, that 'Our kind, 'know what we are on about', though worried we are ready any time to perform on stage, and Succeed, so they with 'Jealousy' crush us before we can evolve. 'They hadn't crushed me, though slowed me down',* **"Better Late than Never",** *is the saying, because with practical experiences gained with our journey travelled, we are of those who really deserve the 'Diplomas', with the passion to get to where we are going, we will get There, standing Strong, like always. God has a place for all beings, 'GREAT Or Small'. Remember!, 'It's* **what you make of it**', *though, Do it the Right way, or don't do it at all, if it means hurting others in the process.*

Grade 4, it had to be one of my most Strenuous years of my life, if it wasn't enough with the many dramas i had indulged, the course of nature adding to my Grief. I had tonsilitis, followed by an operation, remembering how painfull it was, i couldn't swallow for days, with the taste of blood in the back of my throat, then having returned to the Hospital, to have the doctor pull at the Chunky leftover pieces, and 'Stitches' with long Tweezers and me in great agony. If i had gone on Excursions with the school, to the swimming pools, to then later realising i had a hole in my ear, because if i would swim under water, i would feel sharp pains in my Ear drum, resulting in migrane to an unbearable level, with continuous drilling pain, and everlasting squeeling whistle penetrating into the centre of my Skull, later to be in and out of the hospital, on regular check ups, remembering i had to, tilt my head to one side, and have warm oil poured into the ear canal, in order to help melt the wax to fill over the hole that was causing the Nausia, and stomache aches, i can't forget the swimming pools as i had a little yellow box, the size of the jewellers, when selling a ring, though this box stored two ear plugs, that i wore each and every time, before entering the pools, to prevent the water reaching my ear drums, which caused the pain if pressured by water.

One day i had been sitting with Mark, and in my hand i had held a 'Pacer Pen'. It looked like a pen, though, you pull the back of it, until it seperates from the body, then fill it with lead pencil, the thin type. Silly fool i was, always experimenting,(Unexperienced and unaware) as i put a needle in the front end, with it jamming in the teeth area where the lead should be. Their had been a problem with it, and if you pulled the back off, it whould shoot the front end to a distance of, minimum 2 metres. The plastic threads had worn from time, as the tip had been metal, and it seemed that it had been screwed on, though off balance, destroying the threads, anyways, i hadn't realised at the time when Mark was fighting me for it, when all of a sudden it shot straight to the buttocks of Mr Graham. ('This was not his best day', as he had entered our class room ever so Grumpy, and his hair had been very messy. I remember clearly, as i overheard some other students whisper, "**He must've had a fight with his Lawn mower**", and here i am, always making the crowd Laugh, most of the time accidentally, or from being clumsy), he then jolted in surprise, pulling it out, then without a second or two passing, right after analysing the situation, he then walked over to me and Mark in Fury, grabbed us both by the shoulders, pulled us out off our chairs, directing us to, Yep, you guessed it, "Main Office", everyone started 'oohing' at us and laughing, then 'Mr Graham', silenced the class, ordering the students, "**I don't want to hear any trouble as i'm gone**" he said, leaving one of the students in charge. I was done for.., with today at home being the Hottest days in Hell, i copped it from Mum, Mariah, then returning from work, my Dad.

Mark and I, were not allowed near eachother any longer, we would sit on far ends of the classroom apart, with Orders from the Headmaster, as we simply could not get along, always acting Unorthodox, in a Catholic School.

This Had been the last year attending.

Grade Four, 'The story of my Life'..

CHAPTER 10

Two years of School Happiness

Time to shift schools again, as my Brother had also dealt with an episode ending off in hospital, causing more grief to the large list of humiliations. I could remember the Ambulance being called to School one evening, as i later arrived to the scene, in the yard, with students gathered around a person who was lying on the ground, i couldn't see at the time, and as curiosity killed the cat, i had to find out what was going on, and who it was, i manouvered around the taller and older students, to then find out it was my brother on the ground; i didn't know what to think, though their was a lot of comotion. I thought that he had a seizure alone, though, 4 years later i had found out that Tom and Joe, had grabbed my brother, mocking his disability, and entertaining the crowd like Clowns do, as they were liked for their Stupidity.(They are just Lucky i was young, otherwise, i may have been in Prison for Murdering them both, as with my history, it was easy for me to say, i had nothing to live forward to in life, so let's go 'Bash their Skulls in', Everyone should thank God, i hadn't evolved Yet, other wise i would have made my first wrong towards Failing points in Life). They then stood Thomas upside down, locking his head in between their knees, and feet in the sky, then crunching him to the floor head first, then his seizure

54

commenced, as everybody who had witnessed had kept the matter hushed.. 'Though, What goes around comes around is the saying'. 6 years later the elder brother, Joe, had been Knifed, and stabbed Severely, almost losing his life, though, he met me later on in life after his recovery, with a bump in on the streets, and had apologized to me, as i had mentioned to him of me knowing what he had done to my Brother, and **"You must be one of the luckiest people, being that my brother survived it, Otherwise, i would have Shut your eyes long before your time"**, he replies to me, **"Your a good person Paul, but i wouldn't blame you if you did just that, i was a fool and have done many bad things"**, he could not even look me in the eyes), i could see he was suffering in his life.

Grade 5, i was now attending a new school, though, back in Mariah's life again, to be disgustingly hated every morning as we would walk to school, she would always hurry me up by nudging me on the shoulders; we would cut through the oval of her school, to get to the school i had been attending, 'Sunshine Heights Primary School', though, that 10 minute walk seemed forever, as a Thousand words of hate had been spoken, Suppressed before i could reach school. This was my first day, and she had coached me Thoroughly before entering; **"This is your little sisters school, now don't make trouble, and don't even think to Humiliate the family, otherwise your going to cop it".!** she then added, **"I mean it 'You Ungrateful Spoilt Brat". "Your not the Boss of me"**, i whimpered **back at her** as we reached the School crossing. The crossing lady had been accross the street, and Mariah Quickly added, **"You heard what i told you, you even think to stuff up here, i'll 'Knock your Block off myself"**. I don't really know what that meant, though, i quickly ran across to the other side, right after the crossing lady blew the whistle, i kept running, then Mariah calls me back saying crossly,

"Where do you think your going?, do you even know where your going to be?", "I will find it myself i screamed at her". She then growled at me in a low voice so knobody could hear her, **"Get your pitiful self here, first we take Joanna to class, then we go together".** **"Your the Pitiful self",** i then threw back at her. She then Smirked at me replying, **"You don't even know what Pitiful means, you little Ingrate, now shut up and follow me".** So naturally i shut up and followed her in hate, thinking to myself that i hadn't even begun yet, and she's already making my first day at school crap.

We had walked Joanna to her class making sure she got there safe, as she was still young. (I'm another story, with different treatment), Mariah said **"You wait here, and don't move until i come out, 'You got that', stay here".** After that had been arranged by Mariah, she then returned closing the door on her way out, nudging me with a directional force to proceed down the hall, turning me right holding onto my shoulder top, as a 'Peg' on the clothes line, into another hall towards the principals office. She walked over to the reception, asking for directions to where my class may be; we then moved onwards to my class, with my sister knocking on the door, she then entered walking towards a teacher, who had then checked his book to find my name not being their, so we tried the next room, with this being the correct one. I had been shown my desk, as i sat down behind it, with Mariah wasting no time, having her say with my teacher, never to lose a strike, i then realised, it wasn't of pleasant talk, with me remembering her last sentence to the teacher being, *'if i had been mischievous, to have it reported, as i have that history to play up'.* Always having the first word in, to all the new things in my life, not allowing me to cherish or understand, the meaning of Enjoyable; her stubborn, jealous and selfish ways with sadistic thoughts, always finding a way at playing it sly, as if she didn't know, she was destroying me, it was her plan to have me a failure, in order to keep the Throne, the Spotlight.(High and Mighty posture). As i stated earlier, she being the first child, we three youngest then came into the picture, with mothers focus more on us, then without a chance, we would grow up with hateful games.

(She still until today, speaks against me, and i don't mind at all, as i feel nothing but 'Numb', and learnt to proceed setting goals ahead, learning late to find myself again.

'Through the dark tunnel, i continue to walk; 'Without a fight, i Shan't get there'. I am the only who can cure myself from Mental disease, and i see the light, that guides me to where i need to be, i am there already, though i just can't get get a grip on it yet, as it being so close to touch, though, i am in need of a Boost - and within myself i continue, 'Restoration', in need of a 'Saviour', towards myself, and this Uncontrolled Behaviour, it's all a test, with a lesson to be learnt, and if i don't heal soon, then the people i Love will get Burnt.. 'All Missions are Possible'.! Never say Never!

Grade Five went by Pleasantly(at school). I made new friends, with the teachers giving the students the chance to unfold, learning of inner desires towards proffesions liked, because i can't remember getting myself into any trouble with the Law at school, only at home would the Law be 'Ever so Suffocating'.

The School was located, in a happy climate, Tall trees surrounded it, and the design was spacious; the front of the school is where you would find the childrens adventure play grounds, with a 200 meter length of Athletic toys, such as a Flying fox, Monkey bars, Swings, Sand pit, Spider web dome, Slides, Benches with chairs, long logs lifted a foot off the ground used for Gymnastics, and much more, it had been a joy for any child to attend this school. The middle of the School yard was 'Tar coated', and mainly used for Volley ball,

Netball, Bat Tennis with the Rackets made of thick wood, but the middle part of the school was mainly used for Assembly, we as students were gathered together for, our regular announcements, which could be sometimes boring, especially if it had been to lay down the penalties with strict laws. Often the elder students would bully the younger children, and use their section for non recreational benefits, dissalowing peace to the youngest. As for others, who would jump the fence during lunch break to sneak down to the shops, being only 100 meters away, teachers would always see students passing their time there, where is, our school had it's canteen, though already at young age children smoked cigarettes, and hung out where they thought was cool.(at the shops in front of the high school Group). Besides those boring announcements in assembly, i can remember all the sports i had competed in, with Tennis being my favorite.

I remember having quiet a few friends, 'Timmy H', who we first met eachother bumping and calling eachother names, though we became friends. I Knew he had a crush on one of the Goergious looking twins, 'Linda & Tracey', you couldn't tell them apart, except if you had them both together. As one day 'Linda' had complimented me on being nice, and Tommy happened to notice this, though i knew he liked 'Tracey', as he had mentioned this to me earlier, i saw how he would tease her, and joke with funny and annoying tales. (boys will be boys, i don't think i felt that way that, but Timmy had been much more forward in those areas, as i hadn't even known what a kiss was, he did, and the things that would come out of his mouth, make me wonder sometimes). (In a way, after he had finished with me, speaking from his knowledge, In mind, 'I wasn't virgin anymore'). I couldn't reply to him, i was dumfounded with shyness.

Timmy and I would often play 'Minnie Football' under the cover way, right outside our classroom, though, this inparticular day he played Butcher, and that's exactly what he did, he butchered me to the ground, after wearing his red and white Shin pads, aiming at my lower legs, knocking me to the floor. I stayed down holding my Ankles until the pain eased off., "**what was that for**"?, i moaned at him, "**You know what that was for, i told you i liked Tracey**". Timmy replied "**But, what are you saying, that was Linda**", and i started to laugh at him, he got upset and told me "**Go i don't want you here**", o.k, i said to myself, as i found that he was getting violent, so i walked off to the big covered Tennis courts, and found Nick. He had been a great Tennis Player, and i enjoyed watching him play, though his usual partner had been absent, leaving him without an opponent so he swiftly shouts out, "**Grab a Racket from that bag, and get your sexy ass in here**" he said. So i did just that like their was no tomorrow. We then played until the bell rang. Funny boy, though very understanding and Loyal. It had now been the end of Lunch break, so i quickly helped pack up the equipment, and we rushed off to class. Timmy sat right next to me, with half way through the period we became friends again, he did apologize, then we laughed about how the two twins looked so much alike, with me pointing out the fact being, Tracey being shorter, and Linda having an extra mole on her face, small but noticible if you looked closely enough. I don't believe he butchered me ever again, and every time we encounterd the girls, we would stop and stare to anylize my findings, with a smile of rememberance of our misunderstanding with one another, but we always laughed, as it was our secret story, with a memory to cherish.

Grade five at school went by like a breaze, it's just at home i dreaded the most, as the thoughts would always haunt me, my mind would swell, with after shocks, with flashbacks of the events that took place there; and before i knew it i was in grade Six. I may not have been the brightest student in my class, though i do remember, that appreciation was granted to all Children, with the understanding from all teachers., lots of love to all the teachers in Sunshine Heights Primary School..

Here are some of my most enjoyable or remembered moments during grade six, as i remember one morning arriving at school, finding 'Police officers' who had dissalowed our entering the premises, to then being informed of a break in, and blood spots trailing down our corridor, in most of the building. After the forensic tests performed by Police, they then gave the school a clearance, allowing access to the building, remembering very clearly, as all students entered, as well as i, realising the 'Stink', it was tremendously suffocating, as if something died and decayed, to then see the thick blood stains covering the corridors. The smell of Vomit, and dry blood had been so unbearable to handle, with no more than five minutes had passed, when on the loud speaker, the principal had announced a meeting to commence, in the middle of the school in the yard, and to also collect some books and necessities, so we all gathered ourselves, with approximately Ten minutes later, we had all been seated, in anxiety, waiting for the Principal to have his word.

He then arrived, with he deciding, that it was best for the first two periods, we should stay outside and proceed with our studies; as he felt their had been no need for any comotion, dealing with the matter with his utmost and secured methods. He had given instructions to the Cleaners to thoroughly clean the building, opening all windows allowing those two periods and recess to freshen up the air in doors. I give Credit to this school, as today it still is in Functional Use., 'Good Job'.

I am now in grade six, with it rolling by smoothly, mainly because i hadn't my sister(Mariah) in school destroying my reputation, 'Allowing' the teachers to see me for who i really am. I am sure that all through the years of schooling, the elder people had been around longer realising, i was not the problem of my family, they understanding i was only a child, so what fault can a child be in, if they hadn't the experience to know how to deal with Life, with resposibilities as an elder would, 'actually', children or most of them, would act in good favor more than grown ups could, whilst few elders filling the young minds with unproffesional theories and methods, with a lot more at stake, as most parents not seing or understanding, they destroy the well being of their childs future, with their unexperienced ways, uneducated and careless actions, always looking for the easiest way out, thinking they own their childs thoughts, by trying to program their every move, forgetting they once were children, and most of all forgetting, the child has a mind of their own.

The best way to give a child a happy and possitive mind, is to sit and explain, the 'wrongs and the rights', the 'do's and donts', explaining the outcome of each action, iteract with the 'Five W's'(they have been their for generations) with an easier life to live, though most lazy parents evade a thoughtless task, to happiness without realising, it's much easier to gain focus, with support and love from lessons taught correctly. Their is 'No Excuse', If you 'Love' your children, enough to have them, no matter what's going on in your Life, Good or Bad, *it's your problem*, so deal with it in your own time, and **"DON'T MAKE IT YOUR CHILDS PROBLEM"**, i preach to remind myself, not to become another **Hypocrite**, as i always enjoyed being '**Me**'. I never feared being my True self in front of anyone, theirs no reason to being something i'm not, as majority do, talking uneducated, as this is not **Happiness**.

CHAPTER 11

Ending Appreciation with
unawareness of what's to come

To finish off my last year in Primary school, i remember a half
year semester, when we as grade sixers, had a Program called 'The
Buddy System'. We would all line up outside the grade ones class,
then enter the class room, with then helping the teachers open the
two rooms, that had been divided by insulated folding walls. This
allowed plenty of space for the students to sit spread out, into groups,
allowing every group a distance apart eachother. I had received a
group of seven children, which found me very cool, and i will never
forget that moment, boosting my Self esteem, for as long as i shall
live, which is probably the reasons why, i am who i am today. In my
group i had seven great children. 'Nicholas' a multi talented boy,
very creative, and imaginative, with a character of moment to 'Never,
Ever forget'. For he being over active, and ever so talkative, always
having his word in first, little uncooperative, though, you knew he
was very anxious in achieving, and showing his talents. He somehow
interupted the other children, never allowing their colours to shine,
nor perform, So i decided, as the children in my group could not
concentrate, i must shoosh him up in a way, he must learn to share
and appreciate, others as he would like in return. So i cut in and

forced him to sit down, to start our program. He froze with a sudden silence, i realised his happy mood transform to a sudden questioned look, so i quickly, congratulated him on how he was a smart boy, and then added, **"though we as a group have to prove to other groups, we are the team of the Class, though, inorder to do that"**, i then realising **i** had gained access to all childrens attention, with all ears of interest on how we would succeed on it., **"So, we will have fun doing it"**, i added, then all the children cheered, then again they had become anxious and playfull, looking around for toys, **"But, we are going to do it my way, and we have to work together, but i need your help"**. That's how i got their attention, with an ever so enthusiastic posture, they automatically, sat in a neat circle, sitting up straight in silence, though dying in suspense, and before i could bore them out, i asked for their names individually, and although i had shooshed Nicholas several times politely, he later understood, and learnt respect on his own; We had fun with our educational tasks, with the kids in my group being the happiest, also loud and proud, with then hearing the children in other groups chanting, **"Paul is cool, we want to be in his group, can we go to Paul's Group"**. before this moment that i Shan't forget, the group next to me were moaning, how 'Eva', my class mate, was mean strict and boring. They would get up on their knees, and peer into our circle, as all the children could hear how much fun we were having, though as our time was up, and time to switch groups, was a task itself as most of the children wanted to be with me, it was all Nicholas's doing, as he was the most active of all, the kids just wanted to be 'Happy' having fun, with Nicholas being just that, on the time of group change, he remained in my group, as he had a slight temper, and i would not question his backround, though believe to allow him a place in life where he felt 'Comfortable', being where he 'Wanted'. I don't know why, but in a way, i could feel he came from a neglected

place; '*I Saw Myself*' In his Smile, '*a smile that Hardly ever did*',
and when he did, i Understood one thing, it's not about me, I looked
up at the teachers, and they realised Nicholas was a bit of a handfull,
and i needing a small break, though, i mentioned nothing of it and
played it strong, allowing Nicholas to stay in my group; it was a bad
call for the rest of the children who wanted in on my group. They
questioned with '**why**', followed by complaints, '**that's not fair**',
'**why does 'Nicholas' get to stay in 'Paul's Group'.?** I felt ever so
guilty and helpless, wanting then, all the children in my group, as i
realised their sad tone of voice, but i'm sure they were o.k after that.
I'm pretty sure it had been better for Nicholas, as during that year
in the playgrounds, he would often find me if in the yard, informing
me of his problems, and ofcourse i would sit and speak it out with
him, to come up with a solution., i tried my best, being careful of my
words as he mentioning that other classmates found him unbearable,
and how he had zero friends, thanking me for being his friend.

Our task as elder students, were to play a role model figure type,
to help the young interact, and teach us to bond with the youngsters
to feeling comfortable amongst others. We would teach a variety of
lessons, which consist of mathematics, english, Games, etc.., i don't
know exactly what the whole deal was at the time, as i never really
paid much attention, in class, not for the reason i had been naughty,
as i hadn't been at all; mainly because of the clouded thoughts left
in mind from what had been going on at my house. I can tell you
one thing, in a way i lacked concentration during class, i surely and
must have learnt all i need to to know, as sub consciously, i remember
today, the lessons spoken in class all through my schooling Career.
Even if the teachers thought i lacked that concentration, or said i
hadn't been smart enough., they had been wrong.! Their had been
times in my adult years where i'd get stuck, looking into an educated
solution, i would remember lessons in class, as if it were yesterday,

then find the answer to my problem, with the ability to proceed in life. So i really believe in school and don't think, if i had the chance to turn back time, i just know my education would have been the same as it was back then, so i would not change my educational aspect; i'd just disqualify the humiliating features concerning my family issues, published each year of my life in schools. *I should think i did the best i could, and thank the Lord that it was 'I', who dealt with this pressure*, as their is knobody that i know, who had been abused in this manor being tolerant, or nowhere near as strong as i to proceed in life, without becoming a killer, or entering prisons giving up on my surroundings., though, i too felt lost and crazy, to a point where i had decided *to take my own life, further on into the future at the age of Fifteen; as it was the thoughts of failure, under pressure, feeling the Hate in my House. It had been ever so unbearable to be living in this life, not appreciated or complimented, I felt like dying, "so who would want to Live". Thanks to one of **Gods Guardian Angels**, who on my last breathing seconds, saved me from **My 'Sin' to be**; to be of the **'Weakest' Souls,** to take their own life, as to give up without a fight. Ofcourse, It didn't happen, this man changed my view of life and people, because he used words expressing 'Life', and 'Importance', he had controlled me, with only an hour and half of his time, never to see this man again, though i had his voice guiding me, always asking myself, **"What would He Say or Do"?**, i would try to think his way, all would end in a rationalized manor. 'Bless you Sir' for the lesson that remains 'Loyal', and 'Logic', which has kept me up to date with myself remaining 'Sane' wherever you may be..*

Grade six ended gracefully, and fast, without recalls on any mishaps, as those two years at this School, had gone by without much of an acknowledgement..

CHAPTER 12

Introducing my humiliation

It was time for the 'Big One', 'Year Seven', moving up closer to the elders, and more to Mariah.

Now being older, though, still unaware of the real street taste, and how people really were, when in independent mode, i hadn't known what that meant, i had been controlled all my life, so deciding for myself, was a difficult task at hand. I would panic for years with lack of confidence, in order not to stuff up, because a picture in the cloud above my head, would always pop up, with a vision of Physical Dicipline dealt with from Mum, Dad, or Mariah.

Their are alot of cruel people out there in the world, *('in my world' i only saw what had been going on at my house, those involved 'Were the bad people', and all that had been taught, every day as a constant reminder, "The People are bad out there, So Stay inside until your old enough, i don't want you going out of the house, the people are not good out there, i don't want you becoming like them".)* Mariah would always barge in the middle of a disussion, referring to decisions wether or not on letting me go to the park, she would selfishly say, **"Don't let him go, he's spoiling the family, the little selfish brat, it's not fair you let him go, what**

about the others". She'd only say that in laziness, not wanting to show her face with us, in Shame.

(yes, what about the others, the park is across from our house, if you really cared for the others, and not ashamed, you would take the others to the park aswell, because my little sister, and Thomas would also like to go; 'let us out of this 'Cage'), but i didn't have the mind to tell her that, as all i wanted was to be free, it was too suffocating in this house, i just wanted out, in desperate need of fresh air, to play sports, ride a bike, run around, kick a ball, associate with others, what children do best; 'Our best' here at home, lessons taught Hate..

Other than those who had me trapped, and believing, i was worthless. I had been deprived from the street life, exercising my people skills, though, i grew up being gullable believe in the lies, that were promised to be of true nature. (heavy mistakes were made, then i understood later into my adult years, It clicked in mind, though it had taken me my whole Lifetime to figure out how to overcome, or shake off all the suppressed Psychology, forced to live others incompitance, with no intensions of real interest, wanting a peaceful life, though don't know the right way to deal with happiness, lacking the neccasery qualifications, and damage another without a rashional thought to consequences, only to evade in denial, where is, they may be the cause of grief around, but placing as it seems the fault elsewhere).

Being away, from close contact with my family, all other people seemed friendly to me, and that's how it was, i spoke to almost any one with concerns, and feelings, with interest towards helping, and i helped many who were feeling down, going through a rough patch in life, instantly forgetting about my own situation, fitting in time for another in need; everyone who encountered me, were sure to leave, with a piece of me, with a reminder, never to be forgotton, as i always have this thing to teach from my findings, for others to learn sooner, as i would learn, i would share the knowledge of experiences without hesitation, nor selfish or greedy.. (after all that's how i entertained a sad or boring crowd, with stories from my experiences and findings, keeping myself away from unwanted chit chat which involves backstabbing others, my motive had only been beneficial to all).

During this year settling in, meeting new faces, making new friends, having trouble with some students, such as bullies, normal things in the life of a school, i always tried my best not to interfere with Mariah, not going close to her knowing of her character, 'Ashamed' and 'embarrassed' to introduce me as a family member, or if somebody found out of me being her brother, she would quickly turn to her friends and pronounce, **"Oh, this is The little Ungrateful Thing, the little pest of the house"** as she found me next to the Library collecting a volleyball at lunch break, she blasting me why i'm on this side of the school yard, like she owned it, and that moment she felt nervous of people finding out of our relations, i witnessed her explaining to her mates, that i was the destroyer of her life. I don't know what happened to her in life, for her to be so cruel, but i know that when you have jealousy, or when your afraid, embarrassed, selfish, and stubborn, trouble follows. Later on after school, Mariah would make it an issue, announcing at the kitchen table as father would be home at that time, **"and tell that little Brat to keep away from me at school, i'm sick of the little Dork"**, and all i had done was chase the ball from the volleyball court, down the sloped yard, which entered the Oval passing the Library. Mariah had felt threatened by my existence, disowning me with hate, always acting an image of the opposite, of who she really was..

Thomas was also attending the school, which made things even difficult for me, students picked on him for having a disability, then they would pick on me, also the fact, Mariah did a good job of humiliating me in front of people. Though behind her back, most of the oldest students had always commented on her Fake image, and bad character. They would always say to me, to do what i liked doing, and not to listen to her, because she's to 'Bossy', and wants every thing her way. Their had been lot's said against her, though, school hadn't been my major problem. Mainly behind the doors at my home, where the powerful abuse took place.

Friends would start coming over to my house. Remembering, 'Robert', he entered our home, and my mother made us sit in the lounge room, Four meters distance in close range view, keeping a sharp eye on us, making sure not an ounce of mischief during homework took place. We could not concentrate, as All members of my family were making too much noise, I then asked Robert, if he wanted to transfer our books to the dining room table, where we had peace and quiet?, my mother heard me, with a quick jolt in reflex, she shouts out, **"NO, YOU STAY RIGHT HERE WHERE I CAN SEE YOU".,** humiliating me in front of my friend.

Robert didn't expect that, he jumped in fright from mums sudden loud voice, he then decided to pack up and leave, right after he had placed his books in his backpack, he rushed to the door swinging it opened, and said, **"i will see you tomorrow at school Paul, bye"**, the door shut and then my mother started shouting at me, **"YOU ARE IN MY HOUSE, AND YOU SIT WHERE I CAN SEE YOU BOTH, I DON'T KNOW WHO THAT BOY IS, OR WHAT KIND OF A FAMILY HE COMES FROM"**, she raved on. I was so upset, i swiftly turned to her and said **"Roberts in my class, and he's my friend, and he came to study"**. Mum quickly adding, **"Your to young to know who, or what a friend is, and don't give me that rubbish, he came to study, do you think i'm stupid"**, I won't answer that!, though, that day all students paired up in class, with our task being after school to meet up and revise our homework together. "NO, I'm the Stupid, who even thought to bring friends over to our house. I had then left the room, and found myself in my bedroom in fury. I then could here loud talking, being my sister poisoning my mother with false accusations of Roberts cousin. I silently crept closer to listen in, and heard Mariah saying, **"his cousin, called me a bitch in school and thinks he's a big shot, i suggest to you to tell your stupid son not to go near Robert, that families spells Trouble"**

Actually Roberts Cousin was a Cool bloke, he shook my hand, and spoke to me like a gentlemen, my guess is Mariah with her High and mighty fake character, didn't get her way with him, and with her 'lies', he resulting in fault, because, in my experience, majority of the Guilty people that have sinned in front of me, always place the fault on others in denial.(Make Wrong look right and vice versa)

Robert did not sit near me in class the next day, nor did he talk to me, it was more like he had been 'Avoiding' me. I knew the reasons why, though i had that feeling inside where i felt like asking him 'Why'?., anyways, i didn't.., well, could you blame him.., 'No', but i understood him, though it hurt me even more, that i had a friend, who was afraid to even look at me, encase my mother was a Killer or something. Every time he looked at me, i could see he felt sorry for me, which made me even weaker, feeling as a person who has lost his dignity, i felt worthless and damaged..

Half way through the year Robert and I met in the school yards occasionally, feeling safer in the school grounds, he mentioned to me, **"If we were to meet with eachother, then it would have to be at school",** and so i agreed with him, because i was a happy that he wanted to even be my friend. So we continued our friendship throughout our high school years.

Sooner through this year, every one became well aware of each other, and i hadn't an option, but to take whatever came my way. People found out my brothers condition, ambulance would arrive at school Several times a year, as he would have seizures on school grounds, letalone, on occasions i heard bullies would find him and heavily thump him out, but, 'no witness's' would talk. I would get called a retard for many years, pushed, tripped, fights, arguements, more and more people took advantage of me, and the more agressive i became. For the two years i had been in the school Mariah attended, she did a good job having us the Laughing Stock of the decade, and i fell into the trap, adding more to the crisis, as i didn't have a clue, how to deal with myself, i had been drifting, further and further into the land of, **'Who the Hell Cares, i Just Want to be Free'.** So naturally, i gave up interest, and every day mum would be at the School, for either, i was missing from it, or for fighting in the yard, or in the mornings if Mariah hadn't walked us to school, mum would drive me there, park her car in the teachers Car park, then walk me to the principals office, and until we arrived to the main entrance, half the school had witnessed Mum holding me by the hand like a child, soon enough with everybody pointing and laughing at me, as i would be the only teenager at school who's mum would walk with them to class. You could hear the students in classrooms as i passing, mocking me out aloud, **"Oh Look, he needs his mummy to hold his hand to class".** People pushed me around, and i feeling that they were a better person than I.., Well i give anything to switch lives with any person who thought at that time, they could deal with this misery, 'Happily' and without interference towards their future.., i was getting really fed up, i just couldn't deal with it anymore, i could not think to keep my head in my books, and to complete my studies, i just wanted the bell to ring, or not to be hastled by teachers, as they soon classified me a lost Cause in Life, not all, but my co-ordinator Mrs Sin, (who was ever so happy to hand out Conduct Cards to me), my maths teacher Miss Cappino, (she, at Parent teacher night at the interview, mentioned to my parents, i was a 'No Hoper'). Ofcourse, when we arrived home, i had copped hours of lectures, being dissallowed to sit on the couch, forced to sit on the floor, **"Sit on the Floor like the Animal that you are"**, my mother would shout, then she would hover over me, screaming with splats of spit showering me, about my future, how she can't take it anymore, she'd scream at my father, as it being his fault, and if i tried to sit on the couch, she'd grab me by the ears, and pull me down to the floor, and my father, who people would say is a good man, just stood their watching, allowing mother to Psycologically destroy my self esteem, One hour later, you would see dad nearly closing his eyes on his sofa, and mother is still blasting me, thinking that i've been Diciplined after that episode., 'I should think not', it just gave me another reason to dislike you even more, and i had never felt so dizzy in all my life, ready to faint, or die and go to heaven, **'I wished at that moment i had never existed'**. Mum could see that i was exausted, and sleeping on myself, unable to keep awake from Suffocating Stress, i felt **'Lifeless'**.., that was it, i was woken by dad and he realised i couldn't move, as he picked me up in a struggle, he must've understood, i hadn't been at all well; i woke the next morning to find myself in bed, not remembering how i got there. It had been a fairly quiet morning, nobody said a word to me, until after school, when all was forgotton, and the problems they had, where then forced on me, Again. Every day the same old routine, though every day i was growing Nervous and uncontrollable, losing it to a further extent, adding to my tension, i needed to let go, but where?, i didn't know how to deal with myself, i didn't know what to do with myself. I always new what to do with everything, though at this moment, i felt like a person with out a soul, just moving around practising how to feel Numb.

CHAPTER 13

Incident with Understanding, and Warning

Until i reached year nine, Mariah moved onto university. Even though she hadn't been there to humiliate me, the damage had already been done and left to Haunt me. I was well known, amongst those few who just lack motivation in learning. Always mixing in bad crowds, I Love learning, though i couldn't learn., I would always have the thought of mother entering the school coridors, checking classrooms, looking for me to make sure i had attended Class, and not 'Wagged' school, again.

There was the final straw for me. One day she decided, to enter my 'Social Ed' class, i heard the door rattle and could here someone walking in the corridor, and through the glass fitted on the door i could see, my mothers hair, 'shit' i said, and no more than 'Three seconds i flew to the window of the classroom, opened it, and in a flash i was out and running, i ran and ran until i knew i was in the hiding. Just before the school gates their were some nice bulky bushes, i quickly hid behind them, and just sat their thinking, i don't care if i get in trouble by the school, i just could not face another humiliating moment, moaning at myself, for being a 'Mess up'.., **'For crying out loud, what do i have to do for some leaniancy'?**. Five

(5) Minutes had passed, then you would here the school Microphone, **"Paul' to report to the Main Office.., I repeat, 'Paul' to report to the Main Office".** *'In your dreams i said to myself'.* First we let my mother drive out of the school, so i know i'm safe, besides i felt i needed that break, the loud speakers repeating once again, though i did not budge, i sat behind the bush that protected me from sight of humiliation, no more than two minutes later, i see my mother on the other side of the yard, walking over to her car, she stopped and took one glance towards my way, then she entered her car, i started to panick, as she drove outside the gate peering in, it looked like she saw me, but she may have been looking towards the far end of the school in hope to catch me. She drove off, and i let out a sigh of releif feeling Grief, though ever so happier i had outsmarted her for the first time. I now decided after 15 minutes absent from class, i should return to before the period ending; i opened the doors to the corridor, and couldn't believe it, things were normal, nobody in sight, and my class was on my left beside me, so i walked over to the class door, i didn't bother knocking, i casually opened the door and walked in, i sat at the table where i had left my books. Everybody, was surprised, though keeping their cool, as if it never happened, keeping me in suspense, on what was next on the list of 'Torture Paul List'. Surprisingly, **'Mr Law'**, my social ed teacher, welcomed me back, evading negative vibes, Saying in a friendly tone, **"I would like to see you after class if you don't mind"!** **"Yes Sir"** i replied.

Little did i know, at that same moment, the 'Principal' of the School had been on the telephone reporting this matter to the **'Authorities'**, treating this case as a 100% *'Child Abuse'*.

Until tomorrow, i hadn't the faintest idea that i hadn't been in the clear yet. Right after Mr Law had mentioned to me, to stay back after class, he stepped inside his office, closing the door behind him, no more than half a minute later, he smoothly walked back in the classroom, standing in front of the blackboard, asking everyone to put there books away, as it had been time for the bell.. The whole class had been silently talking amongst eachother, as Mr Law made it clear to all, not to misbehave. He then opened the classroom door, leaving towards the Main office. He was a liked teacher, so everybody was 'for a change', were on their best behavior.

Matthew sitting next to me, who was famous for making funny remarks about anyone and everyone, surprisingly, asked me in sympothy, if i had been alright, i didn't know how to answer to him, because it wasn't like him to care enough to ask a deep question, as i expected him to say *'Hey mummies boy,* or *'Retard',* *'Wog'* also his favorite, *'Fag'.* This changed everything between our friendship, and from that day on, he protected me from anyone who pushed me around. Matthew hadn't remembered, as i had my Kindergarten photo of the whole class, and he was in it., again for the second time being classmates, though a real friend in school; *'Cheers my man',* i hope your doing fine wherever you may be'.

The bell rang, with all students packed and out of their seats, they then left in an orderly fashion, leaving me behind. I didn't fear Mr law, as he understood alot of things about my family, especially being a teacher of this school for many years, he had taught Mariah, knowing her Character, and my brother Thomas, then, here i am. So it doesn't take 'Einstein' to put one and one together, to see, their is an actual crisis in need of attending to. He approached the situation carefully, asking me how i was. I hadn't answered his question, though stared towards the floor, then i apologized for jumping out of the classroom window, he grabbed me from the shoulders, squeezing them in a way, showing that he cared for me, saying, **"Don't worry about it, your not in trouble for anything..., your a good kid Paul, though i have noticed your not yourself lately, and if theirs**

anything i can help you with, you know you can speak to me, i'm here for you, just tell me what's going on". I wanted to say something, but just didn't know what to say, or how to say it, so i stood their with my head to the floor, and tears soaking my shoes. He mustv'e been analizing me, trying to visualize what the hell was happening at my house when i would be there.., he then reached for my chin, and said to me to have a seat, **"I can't, i have to be in Science Class"**, i then mentioned. He asked me who my teacher was, then assured me not to worry about Class, to have a free period with him quietly.. Eventually, he had fished out of me all he needed to know, and for the half hour remaining, he spoke wise about his past, and how his parents were good to him, as not all children have that Luxury, me being a smart kid, though he understanding how tough it must be, to deal with 'Physical and Psycological abuse', and it's severity, he asked me to enter his office, where he said to take off my Top. I didn't want to at first, but my option had been, to do so, or i'd have to answer to other members of the School, so i pulled my shirt off, and he could see that it was not only my top half being bruised, i had been whipped from top to bottom, with a thin solid stick, leaving Painfull Blood Blister Whip lashes all over. Now my heart was racing, he said **"Paul you know you don't have to take this abuse, you have to report this to the Authorities, this has to stop"**. He added

"I can't, they will kill me, it's going to be worse if they find out i dobbed them in to the Police". I quickly added, in desperation trying to stop this from happening, though allowing the Truth of the matter to be thrown back at me, with Mr Law waiting to say, **"This is why you have to put a stop to this, if the Police speak to your parents, then they will have to stop hurting you, as they will be punished if they do it again"**.

Then he had mentioned to me that the principal had already called the Police. I started to panick even more, though spoke in force this time, making it clear that he must stop them from apprehending my parents, begging him not to let this proceed..

He could see how scared i was, looking into my eyes, 'Evaluating the Discretion' in my tone of voice, he then Inhaled his tears of concern, with truce, he understood, how severe the situation was, he felt powerless, though a **'Want'** to do something about it, though seeing into the future consequenses, and what disasters may bring on the outcome of rebound.

Their had been a minutes pause, as he held my shoulders thinking to himself, whilst i was shaking in tears; he then spoke guiding me to his chair, saying **"Have a seat here, everythings going to be alright, just give me a minute, i'l be right back"**. I hadn't said anything, though i had in mind to leave and run far away as possible, though i didn't have anywhere to go, besides my Science teacher across the corridor had opened her door to keep an eye on me, being well aware that i may run.. (I could run 12 kilometres non stop in P.E(Physical Education class) as this was one of my best subjects in the School, besides Art).

Two minutes had passed, with lots on my mind. First being, Science class, though after seeing my teacher, i felt she understood, so i new i was in the clear. Sure she new the deal, as my classmates would inform to her of the incident. The moment i had jumped out the class window, the whole school knew of my mothers presence, then with the principal calling for me over the loud speakers.

I had a yellow Attendance Slip, caled a 'Conduct Card', meaning that, each ending period, the teacher in charge would have to sign it, reassuring my attendance, with also commenting on my behavior, and if i would receive a bad comment, my Co-ordinator Mrs Sin, who hated my family, would inspect it. If she found any bad comments, she would happily give me detention. It was Like she enjoyed making me Suffer, provoking the tension in our family, for her satanic minded reasons of enjoyment. Like i said previously, we were the 'Laughing stock of the decade'.

Mr Law had returned, shutting the door behind him. He looked very calm and sure of himself, like usual. He offered me a drink, then walked in his office, returning with a **'Prima'**, that's what we called a small container of juice.

He sat next to me, explaining to me of how he had spoken to the Principal, calming the situation, though, informing me of the Police having kept a Statement of the occuring events, and he making sure that they would not arrive; **"But, if you are a subject to physical abuse, you must report it, as your parents or other members of the family have 'No Right' to lay a finger on you, nor Verbally, and that goes for anyone else in the matter., I also know you are not allowed outside your house, and by Law, you are allowed Two and a half hours as long as you give details to your parents, but don't mention i had told you".**

He then spoke to me of general talk, guiding me towards my rights, and independancy, and reassuring me, that if their was a time i needed to speak to someone, he would be there for me, so don't hesitate to approach him.

(15 years old and i wasn't allowed out the front of my house, i really felt like a 'Doofas', as all children throughout my school career would pick on me, because of my families character towards life. My mother would hold my hand(wrist), when lining up for a school excursion, making sure i get their, (like i couldn't walk myself) in front of all the students, they laughing and mocking me, how embarrassing., or dressing my brother and I in identical clothing all through school career, every one would make fun in all critical terms, killing my self esteem, me feeling embarrassed to show my face. Our house a block away from school, but

mum would drive me there, and walk me to the main office. I couldn't walk anywhere without being called a name regarding my families situation. I always knew that families had their problems, though never met in my days anyone who had My misery, never did i talk to anyone about my situation at home, nor make it a big deal, though i sometimes wished, people who had witnessed what was happening, to help me out alittle, but they couldn't see me suffering inside, with me holding on to my self composure. Their were times though, where i felt i wanted to die, or pictured the three members of my family who had inflicted pain on me, to just 'Die and go to Hell'.

All through my Life, i had nightmares with countless hours of tears, fighting in my sleep, or wetting my bed, getting punished for things that shouldn't be, and i'd even get punished because my parents got punished at young age, and that had been their excuse- 'that's an uneducated excuse if you ask me', and i'm definately sure my parents didn't have us children for the right reasons., Because i'd like to know what was running in their mind if "THE CHILDREN ARE THE FUTURE".

(I Don't care where you come from, 'I Love Life, and most of all i enjoy People', but their's 'NO Excuse' to blame the young and Unexperienced, because as a Teacher, you are to blame yourself for not Teaching well, if your looking for a victim to point and place the faults upon, when life doesn't turn out the way you hoped it would., as blaming is a cover up job from previous mistakes made, knowing at hand when making them, though in denial with yourself, when crap hits the fan, Lies become the Truth, though caring when too late, so it's just easier to throw the dirt elsewhere, destroying the Innocent. That's why the world suffers, from Fakers and Liers destroying others for Self image, jealous, selfish, untrained, and greedy purposes).

The period had ended, as i was leaving the classroom, i turned back, and thanked Mr Law for his time, and apologized for causing a mess in the class. **"Hey, don't even think like that, i just hope one day soon, your family understand, how lucky they are to have a wonderfull person like you in it, so always have your chin up and don't let anyone misguide you.. and don't forget what i said about coming to me for advice".** He looked as if he wanted to say more, as he had a worried look on his face letting me go. **"Thank you Sir, good afternoon".** I then left, and followed the middle yard towards the back oval, which exited to the back street of the school, leading to home not more than a five minute walk. I now am in the park across from my home, i then paused as i saw mothers car driving past, so i quickly hid behind a tree, she slowed down peering into the park, then continued to drive home, i could see the whole street from where i had been, two minutes after she had parked the car in the drive way of our house, i then continued my walk home, slowly. I now reached our letter box, facing the house, savouring the momentary freedom that i had, thinking to myself what would happen when i entered the house, also remembering what Mr Law mentioned about being allowed out of the house, for 2 and a half hours, with acknowledgement from my parents of my whereabouts, and time of return. I then decided to walk, keeping an eye on the entrance of my house. I now reached the door, noticing the curtain moving, within an instance, the door opened to find mother standing their, with her knuckles nudged against her hips, staring at me for more than 15 seconds, she then said, **"Get yourself inside, when your father comes home, then we will see".** I stood there frozen, with visions of dad belting the crap out of me, then mum said, **"Hurry up, get inside".** I entered surprised that i hadn't got slapped, or shoved, pulled, or even shouted at, but i didn't hold my breath for too long, as mum had still given me a reason to worry for. I was feeling lost, this was a big change, i hadn't been abused and i was now standing, thinking if it was a good idea to sit, or will i be expecting in any moment now, a Lecture, or a usual punishment.., damn, i felt empty, what do i do now?. I Placed my backpack on the couch, then walked to the bathroom and washed my face and hands, then i returned back to the lounge room, and sat down near my brother, who had been evaluating the newspaper, occupying my time with watching television, and conversating with Thomas. My little sister had been playing with dolls, and Mariah had been studying for 'Psychology of Arts' on the kitchen table, she had the best of everything, just as she had planned for so many years, and found the best topic to study, manipulating the system with the books, destroying anything in her path, to make only herself happy, 'Temporarily', only caring on how to make people believe, what wasn't and learn others minds, then playing them for fools, and taking money, and lot's of it, cutting me out of the picture. When we would go shopping, we'd only go to follow her. With all the years tagging along, i had witnessed Mariah tricking mother, into spending money on expensive clothing, jewellery, Books worth over 70 dollars for one, and if i had asked to buy a book for my school assignment, Mariah would turn to mum and say, **"No, he doesn't need it, he's got no use for it, he's still young",** then she'd turn to me and poke her tongue out, smirking with a high and mighty posture, proving she had Won the battle. She would always have the first word in, and mother would instantly side her. This evening as she had denied me two books, totaling to 13 Australian dollars, i got upset as it had been part of my essay project, so i stormed off vanishing into the shopping centre(K-Mart), then placed the books in my pants, and headed for the Escalator. I managed to pass the exiting security guard, unaware, that at the top of my ride, had been another Security guard waiting for me, i looked back down the escalator, and found another Security guard looking directly at me, and knew automatically this had not been good at all. They stopped me then walked me to head security.

Eventually, they let me off with a 5 year good behavior bond, as i it had been my first offence.

My sister controlled everything in the house, i wasn't allowed to eat, or drink, only when they would say.

Mariah showered every day, she would tell mother, Thomas and I should shower on a wednesday and saturday, because **"They are Boys, nobody is going to care"**

How about 'I', you think 'I' didn't care. For so many years with the problems you forced upon me, i was ashamed to sit close, or share space with many people, because of the grub i smelt like, because every other classmate, no matter how poor their family were, 'Always' smelt like shampoo, all through the week, So, yes, I Cared). I had been forced to dress the same as my brother, go to bed always at 8:30pm every night, as they would stay up until 12pm, with sundays we being forced to stay in bed until 12, sometimes 1pm midday, until mum decided, it was time to get up, and if i was found walking around before hand, i would get punished, then sent to bed, **"And don't move until, 'i'm' ready, so you better listen to your mother, your spoiling the other children in the house, now go and stay in your bed now, otherwise you will see what i do to you later",** *mum would add.*

5:45pm, i heard the keys, it was father, i felt happy, but, let's just not get to excited now, i still had in mind mothers threat, regarding my father and when he found out, what he would do to me. Though, the event was not spoken for, as she knew, she had been the blame for what had happened. I don't think she even spoke to Mariah about the matter, because this evening had been easy for me.

A couple days later, normal routine of agression had taken place again, broom sticks breaking over me for going out to the backyard when dissalowed permission, and slaps in my face, pulling of my ears, whipped heavily by a solid but thin wooden stick, shaped as the front end of a billiards Cue stick, shoes thrown at me, and at mothers and fathers absense, Mariah would slap and pull my hair, because i would not 'Obey' her. i could not take this anymore. What ticked me off the most was, that my father would give me the heaviest of beatings, only because mother or Mariah had brain washed him into doing so, though that's no excuse either, as the right minded person would not lay a finger on their loved ones. He also belted my mother to the floor, when i had been at the age of thirteen, she had pressured him, pushing him to his limits, he losing control, and i remembering my mother out of breath on the floor crying, **"Don't you hit me again, or i will call the police, you Animal"**. These were the methods of dicipline back in homeland, and they thought i deserved the treatment as they did, because i wasn't any better than they, as just before the beating they would mention, how they would also get the belt for being in the wrong or right. So why should you get the special treatment.

Mariah had run away from home a couple years before, but prior to that, i had followed her to her friends house where she ran to, as they were best evil buddies at school. I had been their for just a moment to listen to her friend Mary saying to Mariah, **"Big F..n deal, our parents made us, but they don't own us, don't care for them, take them for what they have, we didn't ask to be here, and they havn't done anything good for us, they only destroyed our lives"**. Mary's dog started to bark, so i quickly got up and left, running towards home as it had been 150 metres down the street. This is where Mariah picked up her bad habits from.

Mariah excused her reasons for running from home (for jealousy and selfish reasons), concerning us brothers and sister, can't stand this house of incompetents. She just wanted the attention to be focused only on herself, and despised the fact we were in this life, cramping her Goddess style.

Please excuse my Sarcastic Character, *'I Promise to all, as a witness 'He' who has the 'Power' to Condemn me to Hell if i'm Lying'*, though i'm not this kind, and sure don't find it in my heart to inflict Pain upon others, unless in 'Self defense'(Matter of Life and Death situation), other than that, i 'Despise this kind of 'Cheap play', from 'Foul minded sore Losers', and should think the 'Culprit' feels the same, though i'm not playing, and never had been, and surely don't intend to, so if i feel this strong about helping others, how is it possible?, for others to not even feel a slight bit of remorse by their actions, (These kind of people walk amongst others looking and talking Sane- Blind mans bluff, if i should say) watching others who suffered enough, to persue a goal of 'Total destruction' towards their victim, even when they are not present, the years of torture to the Victim 'REMAINS A CONSTANT TORTURE HAUNTING THEIR WELL BEING TO LIFE'

CHAPTER 14

Standing my Voice

These last years of my school career, had been very difficult to concentrate on passing exams or focus on studies, as my main focus without a say in the matter was on punishment, always in the back of my mind, i would worry with constant visions and flashbacks of how or with what tool next i would receive torture. Friends would not even come over to my place, as the word got out, of how suffocating it really was entering my home. Anyone who would come over to study, would not even sit near me in class the next day. Mum would interogate my friends, leaving me with friends being afraid to even being friends with me. Students would backstab me to the teachers, informing of the conditiions i lived in, soon the 'Whole' school knew of me, and if things wern't bad enough, my mother decided to send a substitute teacher 'Mrs Blunt', who had been helping my brother with his progression in school studies, all through the years with his disability, she had asked for her to attend to my aid just like Thomas, as if this was my problem with my lacking of concentration in class. I made it clear to 'Mrs Blunt', i did not want her next to me, as i knew she was well aware of my families condition, allowing her to understand, that i wasn't to tolerate, any more 'Psychological Disturbance', **"And i'm not going to tell you again, or i will run**

away and never come back", so she hadn't interfered with me again. I hadn't needed guidance, as i would recieve scores of 10/10 for Arts and Crafts by a very supportive teacher Mrs King, who i liked very much, as she appreciated me in her class, Bless her soul. I loved Drama, with the principal as our teacher at times, he spoke to me like an elder should, always boosting my confidence and allowing my talents to shine, always smiling in our class. Textiles class was great, i learned how to use a Sewing Machine, painting T-shirts with the squeegy + roller paint set, stitching with a needle. Music, so much fun, especially when entering the back room playing the drums. I loved Computer studies, in that 45 minute time period, as i would occupy my time on the Commodore 64(Old skool) playing a game called Space Buggy, i found peace within myself here. Science was an interesting subject, learning the Bunsen burners, blowing glass tubes into Flasks, donating insects to the class museum, and disgustingly disecting a rat, and naming it's organs pinned on a board. I still can remember that pong of a smell it had 20+ years ago, Electronic technologies was one of my specialties, as i was a creator, and inventor, always finding creative ways to make something work with a battery source, such as learning how to power a 6 volt lightbulb with potatoes Beer, or lemons.

The Final Straw for everything, the day had come where i had lost all faith in family Trust, and hadn't cared any longer what was to become of me, as my physical Education teacher, 'Mr Fit' had mentioned to my mother how, i was the best runner in school, running 12 kilometres non stop and knobody could beat me, i had great endurance, and if i was allowed to run more i could, as i being Super fit, Mr fit adding he would like for me to proceed to the 'Melbourne Olympics', helping me with a sponsor, though first of all, sign me in with recomendations on how i stood a great chance of success. But Ofcourse, mother cuts him off screaming at him, **"I don't want him learning the easy way out, he can do it by the books"** Mr fit paused, though enthusiastic with my talent, he approached with another attempt explaining, **"you have to understand, and put in perpective your son has a gift unusual, please give him a chance"**. 'Big mistake', she being to hard headed and selfish, shouts at him ever so abruptly, **"I am his mother and i know what's best for him, and i don't want you filling his mind with wishfull thoughts"**, she then stormed off, and i looking at Mr fit, could see his face, he looked ever so baffled, he must have been thinking, that any parent who had a child with this chance and opportunity, would say 'Yes' within a heartbeat, without questioning, but 'No, not this parent'. This was a moment I 'Hated' her with all my might and guts, i had been humiliated once again, i hadn't been for books, i was practical, and i loved running, and all my teacher had done, was ask for permission to allow me a chance towards a talent i was made for.. i was so disgusted in myself and what had happened, i walk over to the back oval, and found my friends brother, and said **"Give me a Cigarette".** He then looks at me in disbaleif and replies, **"Don't bullshit me, you don't smoke, who's it for"?** **"It's For me,** i assured him, **i will even smoke it here so you can see".** He flipped the lid of his packet, then handed me a smoke, lit his lighter, and then i puffed, and coughed two times then smoked it. I then explained why i started to smoke.

The day had ended, and when i reached home, i went straight to my bedroom, organised some clothes to dress in, as today their was no stopping me from going to a friends house, i was going whether they liked it or not, and i had no plans to tell them of my whereabouts. I returned to the lounge room, and started saying to mother, who had been sitting on the couch cleaning potatoes with a knife,

'By Law i am allowed outside the house for 2 and a half hours, and you have to let me, 'BY LAW'', i mentioned again, she quickly got out of her chair, holding the knife waving it and screaming, **"Your not going anywhere your staying right here, when i say to go, then you can go".**

"Your not the boss of me, i hate this family, you don't love me, all you do is treat me like an animal, i'm going and you can't stop me". I then reached for the door handle with my right hand, then mother grabbed my left hand, the door opened, i still holding on as she had been pulling me, so i put more force, she started raving on, **"The people are bad out there, you don't know how to take care of yourself".** Then i put all my strength pulling the door opened, then she used both hands, but in her other hand, she held the knife and stabbed me with it, as she reached for a grasp, she noticed she had done so, then we both let go with me being shocked with a burning pain, i looked down to my upper stomach to see blood, then i Skitzed/Flipped even more, then growled, **"Get your hands off me, your the bad people here not outside".** I then walked out fast and slammed the door, with the side window breaking, and made a run for it down our long street, towards the main road, and could hear her behind me shouting out, **"Paul, stop, get back here now, stop, now, i'm speaking to you",** but i just kept on running, faster and faster crossing the main road, she could be heard all the way down the street like a raving Lunatic, and i getting closer to the creek, where one of my mates lived. Little did i know, that they were smoking Cannibas, so i tried a pipe, which had put me to sleep, and i woke up not long later, as my mates mother had made a cup of tea for me, well aware of my situation, she held me like a child of her own, brushing my hair, speaking wise to me. I listened to her, though my mother wouldn't listen to reason, as it was now time to head back home, and when i reached home, mum wasted no time grabbing me by the ear, then forced me to the floor stomping on my legs and furiously slapping me in the face, nudging and kicking and pulling my hair, shouting at me, if i don't listen to her she would give me to the Government, poking into my private parts, not allowing me to sit on the couch, **"then they can do what they want with you, because the government know how to deal with delinquents like you, and it not going to be pleasant for you"**.

I felt tenderized, like what you would to Meat with the tenderizer before crumbing it, i was bruised, and my ears were still ringing, she then started her mouth again, **"Your just like your father, a good for nothing no hoper, where is he now, to see you, he is never at home, he must be with one of his girlfriends, always saying he's working overtime but the money is still the same, you will never amount to anything, just like him, a Loser, 'You Ungratefull Child', just wait until your father gets home, your punishment is not over yet, you sit there until he gets home"**.

Eventually dad arrives home and his first step through the door, realising the broken window, with the Informant of the house not wasting any time, finding the moment to her advantage; father looking tired, hadn't a chance to walk through the door, with his hands full, he then said, **"Not again, why can't i come home and hear good things for you, i havn't even walked through the door yet"**. Mariah followed him all around the house, until she could fill him in with all details, being over dramatic with events supposidly i had been in fault for, as always, not mentioning their wrongs and who really had provoked the matter, she had him cornered with Psychology, mission accomplished and brain washed to the limit where he had excused her, until he changed his clothing. He had then entered the lounge room where i had been brutally beaten, without understanding that mum had punished me severely prior to, he then started on me, then ordered me to stand up, **"I can't"** i replied, **"Why not"** he asked, as he saw me trying to get up, struggling in pain and limp, **"What happened to you"**?, he asked. i could not answer to him as my mother and sister were behind him watching, and playing ever so innocent, with a cross look with reassurance to themselves, with a posture to show dad that i had been the cause of greif, and the trouble maker. He then looked back at my mother with her knuckles, nudged against her waste, with Mariah replying to him, in order to change the guilt, just about to show in their faces, **"Well.., dicipline him.., where not gonna have the little brat run all over us, spoiling the family"**. He was so tired and ever so angry, being convinced that i was to be punished heavily tonight. He went outside for a minute, then came back in, with a thin stick he then whipped the back of my body, until finished the back of my arms, my back, my legs were all covered with double whip lash lines, also being slapped heavily in the face, and mouth.

During this punishment, i had been crying, for him to stop, but he would not listen, and kept on Pelting and pelting and pelting me with extra force. I could taste the blood in my mouth, and feel some kind of liquid like a Paste with blood, though i wasn't sure, because i was trying to shake off a constant ringing sound that i could hear in my ears, though coming from in the back of my head, with a feeling when you dive into deep water, and you can feel and hear the bubbly pressure rushing around your head, the sound of it being neverending. From that day until today, it comes back to me when i'm under pressure, with a 'Dwoooooooooooooooooooooooooo ooooooooooooooooooooooooooooooooooooooooo' sound, giving me 'Migraine, headaches'.

The lines had formed to blood blisters, and i had never felt so Numb in all my life, bruised, abused, 'Psychologically', 'Mentally'. Nodding off, i couldn't keep awake trying my best to do so. My punishment with a beating had ended for the moment, though after this, my mother forced me to stay on the floor, in one place until she gave the order to move. I couldn't keep my eyes opened, my mind was exausted, the only medicine placing my mind at ease had been sleep. I felt like 'Jelly', my legs in so much pain, from mother jumping on them, i could not keep my body upright. I slouched over my legs, i then laid in front of myself on the floor with my head on my arms. I shut eye without knowing, and woke up to a slapping and my mother shouting **"Get off the floor, i didn't tell you to sleep"**. I sat up with my eye lids drooping. I tried with all my might to keep my eyes open but i couldn't, and fell asleep sitting upright leaned against the wall. Roughly an hour later, my father picked me up and put me to bed without wash or nothing, whilst he undressed me, he was mumbling how he was sorry for the punishment, but i would have to learn to do the right thing in the future, as mother was giving him a hard time because of me.. I woke the next day, feeling the lumps and bumps all over, with my bruises stinging, with the swelling burning hot, inflating like a balloon. I couldn't walk normally, even if i tried, i would limp. My mother still made me attend school, but little did she know today at school, Mr Fit had schedueled a 12 kilometre run, not knowing of my condition until he noticed my appearance being exausted. He asked **"Paul, how are you are you, ready for today"?. "I'm not feeling so good sir"**, i mentioned.

He grew suspicious, and being very smart as he was, he knew something was not right, and said to me to go to the school nurse, i then said **"I'll be fine sir, i didn't sleep well lastnight"**, and it was as if had been waiting for my reply, he said, **"If you don't want to go to the nurse, then you have to participate in class activities, so i would like you go to the changing rooms and get dressed for sport"**. He said. So i began my walk through the gym to the changing rooms, trying not to limp, and quickly took of my top, behind me ten seconds entered one of my classmates, he must have seen the marks on my body, without saying a thing about it, he had left with no more than a minute passing, Mr Fit had entered the room, locking the door behind him. He asked me again how i was, and mentioned to me of how **'Child Abuse'** wasn't taken lightly here in our school, and **"I'm going to ask you one time, and be honest with me, because i know that it's difficult living in your house, and the people there don't appreciate the gift you possess, i like you as my student, i know your families history, and am very proud of how you are strong, dealing with the pressures at home, but it's a shame i can't do anything about it, especially how your mother spoke to me the other day, i wish i could do more for you. Now, i need you to take off your clothes, and that's an order, as i beleive your not telling me something".** He then reached for my jumper and i started to panick, though i could not fight with him as he was my best teacher, i didn't want to upset him. He then saw the whip lashes, and was furious with tears in his eyes, i started to cry in fear with visions of the police arresting and placing my parents in 'Jail', i was doomed. He let a minute pass turning his head facing the wall.

I don't know what he was looking at with his back faced to me, though thinking about it today, i believe he had tears in his eyes trying to suck them back in again, before facing me again. He then turned back and saw me like a rain forest tearing all over myself, and said to me to take off my pants, **"Now"**, i slowly pulled them down, and he stood behind me silently. he then said **"Get dressed, your not participating today, you will sit the bench".** So i didn't participate. I sat and watched everyone else until, half way through the P.E class, as the word spread quickly that i had been physically abused at home. I hadn't noticed that Mr Fit had put someone in charge, as he had been absent for a short time. He later returned and called me into the Gym, so i stood up slowly feeling the great pain and agony, and limped to the gym. He put one of the students to stand guard in front of the entrance not allowing anyone to enter. I can't remember what he had said to me, though i remember ending off at the nurses room. She was middle aged, and had thouroughly checked me, detailing every mark found on my body, writing it down in my file. They eventually had me in the corner, having me confessed to all. I had no other option, as the police were on their way, and by the time the nurse and teachers had witnessed the markings on my body, and listening to what had been happening at my house, i could hear some teachers commenting in 'Disbalief' and 'Disgust', on how something like this go on for so long, without anyone knowing or doing a thing about it.

Though, as for two other teachers who left the room, saying to one another, **"He probably deserved it"**, they then laughed in a way they hadn't cared, these were the two who had problems with themselves, as one was my Coordinator, ever so happy to hand out Conduct Cards, and the other had been my 'Maths' teacher, who had mentioned to my mother at parent teacher night, that i was a 'No Hoper'.(God watch over you both, with prayers that the people around you are far from harms way, because with your sly methods, 'Spells Poison'), 'SHAME'. Shame on both of you!.

Information had already been given to the school by other students who already witnessed brutality from my own people, not only that, even the teachers and principal indulging with a glimpse into my life, by mother over the years of entering the school premises, with her attitude, and methods.

The Police finally arrived, getting aquainted to all the details, and then checking my body to find it a 100% genuine, 'Child Abuse'.

They then mentioned that 'By Law', they have to apprehend my family. Now i really panicked with visions of me being belted the crap out of. I teared heavily, and looked to towards the police, and begged them, **"Please don't do this, you don't know what your doing"**. Then the officer said, **"This is out of our jurisdiction now, letalone how serious this is towards your future, so what's best is we speak to your parents and give them a warning.., they must stop this"**.

I wanted with all my Heart for my parents and Mariah to be punished heavily for what they had done to me, though i was too afraid to allow this to happen, as i felt i may not come out of this alive, because i wasn't sure what to expect. I had a bad feeling about their theory, as they wern't the ones who lived in my house, nor have to see their faces 24/7/365 days a year.

I then mentioned in fear, but to try and get them to stop their actions, **"Please, i beg of you, don't do this to me, their going to kill me if they found out i told you"**. Now the police were convinced finalizing their say, **"Paul, are you listening to yourself, this is why we are here, this is the reason why we have to approach your parents, so this does not happen again, because if it happens again, they will be trialled in court, and heavilly punished, it's not fair on you, and it interupting the people around you"**.

I begged them not to do it, but the principal made sure to put a stop to this.

I hadn't been good with reasoning, (and as i write this i should have had my parents sent to court, because i still beleive i would have been the same person i am today, though, it would have been 'Heavenly', if i lived my Life having been allowed to go to the Olympics, to have had encouraging and supportive people in my family, it also would have been nice if they never had laid a hand on me in the first place, and being nice if my life hadn't been put on hold, as two members of my family still, speak against me in order to save their 'Reputation, and Image', in fear that people find out the Truth of who they really are. They say things to make me look like, i don't have a clue what i'm doing with myself, or that i'm the trouble maker. So i'm sure whoever may read my story, will believe me, this is the first time i speak of my life with details to approximately the fullest of details, with Courage now to actually speak about my life, and how i lived it, because we can't all be perfect), Though we can find happiness, even if it means to sacrifise a setback, inorder to live an Honest and Healthy life.

That evening as i had been picked up by mother, she hadn't mentioned a word, but kept eye balling me in disgust through the rear view mirror. She drove to my litle sisters school, picked her up, then headed towards home. Mum silently spoke to my elder sister about the matter in the kitchen, as i had been in the lounge room listening to their whispers. Every now and then Mariah would pop her her round the lounge room door, making sure that i hadn't been eavesdropping, though i needed to know, as this was my only escape finding out my next punishment, and how to evade severe damage. Mariah suspected i could here, so she cut mothers conversation off, telling her that they will discuss the matter later, when we were all in bed. They hadn't informed to my father of the encounter with the police, as he had arrived home. Though he mentioned this month he would be working split shift, and he would be off to work again soon. This was Mariahs advantage to destroy the family completely, with a mission to regain access to her lottery.

8:30pm arrives, It was now bedtime for Thomas, Joanna and I, though tonight i was happy to go, as i was on a mission too. We now were in bed, and Mariah closed all the doors except the main bedroom, limiting the allowance for walking around the house secretly. She then made mother a coffee, then placed it on a tray, beside her. I then could here foot steps approaching me, as i had been close to the main bedroom door listening. I quickly tip toed in a hurry back to bed, and played like i was sleeping. Mariah came into the bedroom inspecting to see if i had been in bed, as i had been the only to suspect of being out of bed. she found everything to be o.k, so she left my returning to mother, and started to confrentate with her. I got out of bed, and returned to my hiding place, in close enough range to hear my sister and mother arranging how to Divorce father, taking him to court, gaining custody of the children and even take the house, threatening him to pay 70,000 dollars, otherwise Mariah would tell the court, mum was suing him for striking her to the floor previously. After i had heard enough, i dashed back to bed, and forced myself to sleep.

Later on i had mentioned to father of the arrangements that were planned, with he sure of himself telling me, **"You didn't hear right"**. I insisted that i'm not lying, and i was sure of myself, but no luck, he was convinced it wasn't going to happen.

I have left alot of events unspoken for, as i may need 36 years of my life to explain everything. Writing this book is a very tiring task indeed, as every day i relive the events, as the scars are always there to remind me, why i am the person i am today, and ofcourse, why i'm not the person i wanted to be. It has been a struggle keeping myself alive, trying to fit in with my surroundings. I was the 'Odd one out', though i had a lot of respect from people, i was always polite, i never used foul language, i never picked on people, I had been bullied, though later on in life i, stood up for those who had been bullied.

Some children may succeed with a Degree who proceed to university, and some of us do not.(I was stopped from school, by my fathers 'Want of his Freedom, and regrets to pack up and leave from Australia, to return back to his Home ground)

As children, It doesn't mean we wern't paying attention in class, or not smart enough, as some peoples inner desires due to circumstances, follow the moment of happiness. I know for a fact of many people who hadn't passed for University, had been smarter than 'the' who had, and they had received Diplomas, though, not in 'Book' sense, in 'Practical' sense, because if you don't touch with your hands, you will never know what it really feels like, inorder to control the Full effect.

Books to many people are boring, so you have to understand why many children drop out of school before their time, despite the reasons of psychologicl intervention, or helping with economical matters at home.

Schools all over the world have to use practical methods to feed the active mind, understanding Circumstances are in all shapes and sizes, in order to suite every ones Criteria. 'It's the saying- Understand even if you don't'. Place an Understanding, there where you don't, look into a case, before judging, and never judge a book by it's cover'. It's mostly important to know the facts before Assumptions, as Assuming is as i mentioned previously, 'The Centre of all failing points'.

I had always been tolerent to 'Abuse' and received a fair bit of it, though i have a saying, *'Don't do to others, what you most certainly don't want done to you'.* i started using this saying later in my Life when i learnt more about 'Carma'. 'Unfortunately' i was too deep into Aggression mode, and did not agree with others who would get in my way forcing the demon out of me, for their self enjoyment towards provoking and mocking me. I got into fights and arguements, standing up for myself, dissallowing anybody to push me around, on my expense involving more Psychological neglagence and pressure.

I remember in the library on one occasion, when the librarians son all through the year had been calling me a 'Retard', who referred to me as my brothers condition, but he wasn't that. I always hated when he did this, as he always walked past me bumping into me, inorder to the knock books to the floor. I tried my best to avoid him, and the more i walked around him, the more he'd make it a mission to hastle me. Because his mother had been the librarian. This day i just stopped in my place, and he walked straight into me knocking the books out of my hands. I stopped and stared at him in Dissapointment, he then turned and raised his hands, approaching me placing his face on mine, i guess he deserved it, though, i pushed his face with enough force, and told him, **"Get your stinking breath out of my face"**. I did not know he having a sensitive nose, as it started to bleed. I had been sent to my Coordinator, who she had then extended my Conduct card for another week, with a suspension from school for three days.

Their had been a boy in my class, 'J.R', who had always made funny remarks concerning my brother, though, always making me the 'laughing stock' of the class. I later witnessed him running towards my brother, approaching him from behind, like you would in an Australian football match, taking a mark for the ball as it coming down from the sky, and a player using the shoulders or back of a player, to catch the ball. He ran with full speed and did the same to Thomas, though in full force knocking my brother to the floor. I then stopped and shouted, **"Hey, Dweeb, i've had enough of you, this lunch break, you be in the oval, and we'l see if you can do the same thing to me, and get away with it, and you better be there"**. I then continued down the corridor, and found his younger brother 'D.R' standing there in the hall next to his locker. I had then mentioned to him what J.R had done to my brother, then D.R replies, **"I don't care about J.R, he's a #?!@%, and a pain in the arse at home, as we always fight. What do you want me to do about it"?,** he replied. **"Good to hear, because this lunch break, i've challenged him to a dual, and i gonna break his face in, because i've had enough of his 'shit'".** I then stated.

Amazingly D.R said to me, **"It's about time somebody kicks his face in, and while your at it, punch his lights out for me too".,** he then shook my hand and walked on.

In class J.R hadn't said a word, as he now had other things to worry about. The bell rang, this was it, i placed my books in my locker, and noticed J.R had dissapeared, so i ran as fast as i could to the oval. I don't know what came over me, but i felt i was doomed in this life, with all other setbacks, and humiliations, i now had to do what i had to do, it was time to give back to the bully, this one time, what he had been doing to me for four years, a taste of his own medicine.

I guess he thought that i gave up, 'but not me', this had to end, and i knew that i wasn't going to kill him, i was just in the moment, i was not strong enough to stop myself, i felt that I should stick to my word. I found him walking fast through the school oval, getting ready to go home for lunch. **"Hey J.R",** i shouted, he turned to see me approaching him, then he stopped, dropping his bag to the ground, and started to mouth of to me, swinging for me, but i had manoevred round his punches, and i pushed him to the floor, and in no time, i had reached his face, with four continous punches to his nose, which had started to bleed heavily, i then kicked him another four times in the stomache, then D.R grabbed me from the back, and said **"Paul, that's enough, i think he get's the message".** J.R with blood dripping from his face started swearing at me, with D.R screaming at J.R, **"Hurry up and go home, or i'l let Paul on you again, and i'm not gonna care this time"**.

J.R kept on swearing at me. I was in rampage mode letting the four years of his abuse, that i held inside of me return in revenge, i tried kicking him in fury, but D.R was a strong boy, struggling to hold me back, screaming to J.R to **"Hurry up and go home, your in fault you Dweeb, hurry up, i can't hold on any longer"**. So J.R picked up his bag and ran home as fast as he could, with d.R then letting me go. He then congratulated me, though, he couldn't let me destroy his brother any more, explainig brothers are family., **"You know what it's like"**, he adding. **"Yes i do"**, agreeing with him, then i asked **"How is it that your a fair person, and he's a moron...?, don't even answer..., i have the same problems at home"**.

He grabbed my hand shook it strong, and quoted, **"Don't worry about J.R, i will make sure he doesn't hastle you or your brother again, and if he does, you make sure you come and find me and tell me"**. He then turned and walked on home.

I can say he was a fair guy, and that day he proved it with 'Reason'.

CHAPTER 15

My Prerogative, my only resort to Freedom

During that last year at school, i had made alot of friends. People had stopped hastling me with their teasing and funny remarks. Most friends were all the independent type, who had also lived 'Tough' themselves, such as their fathers were in prison, or a death in the family, seperations, from being abused with similar setbacks in life. Disorientated minds at time of need to be focusing on school, though neglected with unnecessary setbacks.

My Message to a victim of being Shamed by others. Keep your Chin up, place a goal, plan your Journey towards the 'Unknown', though making and taking each step without skipping one. You will be sure to encounter within time, 'The Future' that you Deserve or had Desired for far so long, worth it, if 'You Earned it with 'Passion' and Productive Intensions, following what you love doing, giving with devotion, Respecting 'Time', with i quoting "Don't wait for a miracle to fall into your arms", though miracles happen everyday, go out and make it happen. Be Yourself without letting anyone detour you elsewhere, as it is the words of jealousy with words of an Attempt to prevent you from succeeding. Have an open mind to your surroundings, 'Be Aware' and ready to 'Learn', 'Learn something 'New Everyday', and until you get to where you are going, always keep yourself occupied towards things that benefit you, and Don't 'Grow Weak', though 'Grow Strong', Listening to yourself with decisions made wisely. Listen to opinions, though if choosing, choose correctly and beneficial towards happiness and Health. Reach out to others, and be Sure others will reach out for You., but don't expect anything in return, unless you coprimize.. Keep Sane!

Life is a lesson with experiences, teaching us steps that guide us with opportunities, options, plans, decisions, but know matter what you do, as a mistake i had made, allowing people to control me with words of shame, Don't ever listen to anyone who had said, 'You will Never amount to anything', or, 'You Can't do that', or "Your not capable", or 'Don't'. Make sure that you follow your Heart and beliefs, because, 'Anyone can do Anything, as long as you put your mind to it', see, if you really want something to happen, then you go out of your way and do it. You give a little - to get a little, You give alot - to get alot.

I Pause for a moment, contemplating to myself, as i try to find a good moment lived, like a food to savour, for as long as you can, although difficult to do so, cloudy past intefere with your desire to move on Healthy and happy, though with courage, as i remind myself of any good times, which allows me access to fresh thoughts, peace and tranquility, as this was my savior to keeping sane. Imagination-creation, which i used more than anything to get bye, these were my 15 and a half years at home living deprived of a happy life. No matter how hard i tried to impress my family, it just wasn't good enough. I wish it wasn't like that, as i am writing of my Journey with 'A view from Anothers Perspective and point of view'.

Tonight had been the night, as i had my mind made up, i could not cope anymore. It either meant, i would hurt somebody, or save myself. I had Run away from home at 10oclock pm, planning this at school with a student who allowed me to stay at his house(Jamie). It may not have been a good idea, as one of the other classmates had listened into our conversation, who secretly detailed everything to his sister, who also had been classmates in high school with Mariah.

I couldn't take it anymore. The night before i had planned the escape, All three members of my family had Physically and mentally, pushed me to the limits. Everyday i would wait for my father to arrive home, not realising until later, that he would listen to others brain washing him, into 'Belting the Hell out of me', as to him it was obvious that i had been a trouble maker, and that was final, thinking that this was the case. I needing him the most to put a smile on my face, but he proved me wrong. He physically slapped and forcebly provoked pain, with this time, only in my face.

Many times he would catch me on my own where knobody could hear, mentioning **"You are my favorite Son, you always will be"**. *But, as his favorite Son, He would punish me with 'Uncalled for Lesssons, 'Inhumane'.*

The root to the problem Lies somewhere, and if i were 'Guilty', being brought into this world by these elder people, then the most i could say to them would be, "Sorry for being here in this Life, or sorry for being your embarassment in life, or sorry for 'Making your life miserable". I must be in fault being the youngest..? yeah, right! I know i should not apologize, as somebody should apologize for their Sins, as i am 'Still' paying for mine, The scars are very dirty, stained into my Body, Mind, Heart and Soul. I feel like damaged goods, like an Apple looking ripe and readily delicious, though inside is rotton and Bad... So, i will tell you what i can do.., "I'll forgive You", i always had and i always will, though get one thing straight, "I will never forget"., as

It comes with the 'Package'. Their's a price to pay for everything you do in life.

Don't get me wrong, as i also read what i write, as to practise what i preach, making sure to myself, not to ever inflict Pain and disturbance towards others, unless needed against Self Defence.(A matter of life and death situation, or Prevention of life threatening events ready to occur).

I do believe of 'Freedom of Speech'., as it being 'Now, My Turn'. I have found the courage to speak without fear, and with 'Time as My Friend Helping me to Heal', taught logic, and wisdom, and doing what's right. I ask other victims, to stand up for themselves, 'The Sooner the Better', as anyone who has been harmed, or the trauma persues in continuation, you have to get away. Don't be late, it's Very Unhealthy for the future. Find a way far from setbacks intended by others, and make it a mission to respect yourself, if you seek happiness.

I had been found, mother approached the front door of Jamie's house, banging on it and screaming for me to come out. Jamie's mother opened the door, then i heard both mothers screaming at eachother, ready to fist fight, with Jamie's mother smacking my mother with a wooden spoon, so i eventually came out of my hiding place and surrendered. Mother grabbed me by the jumper and tossed me towards the car, we all got in and drove home. I had been pulled, then dragged, and pushed to the floor in front of the Sofa. I tried to sit on it, then copped/recieved another smack to the side of my face, popping my ear with a constant after shock ringing tone. The night ended with Lectures of how i would be given to the Government if i did such a thing again, with mother pointing her finger into my privates, reassuring me that the government would rape me if placed in jail. Always threatening me, believing this would put everything in order. She had only given me another reason to 'Feel the weight of hate', and nothing more.

I Believe everything happens for 'A' reason, some oncoming are beneficial, whilst others are mind draining, though whatever the reason may be, we have to go on continuing.. Some of us succeed sooner, than those who succeed Later, as some may not at all, though if everything go's according to 'Plans', with the 'Steps' taken correctly, the day will arrive when you get your feet back on the ground. Sometimes i ask myself if theirs another way to deal with this matter, though i just go on believing, we can't all be successful at once, though if you really want to succeed, better late than never. Theirs a place for everyone.

My Parents eventually Divorced, as i had been 16 years of age. Mariah signed her name in the custody of Mother, as she kept close to Mum with her mission to gain access to the fortune she had planned for so long to take charge of. My brother Thomas, had no option in the matter. Mariah coached him every moment she had found alone with him. She placed in his mind, that father had been a Traitor to the family, even if it were true, that father had a girlfriend during the time of Marriage. Thomas signed in custody of mother, and Joanna the same.

As for me, mother came for me 'Three times' within three weeks, had approached the house as dad had been at work, lecturing me always of how she wants the best for me, speaking nicely to me for a change, **"Isn't it better you come with me? Your father will destroy your life if you stay with him, as he has no courage, or what it takes to be a good father, he's a no hoper, and if you stay with him, you will become the same, that's why it's best you sign the 'Custody Papers', come with me, to make a better life for yourself"**. I explained to mother, **"I hadn't asked for this to happen, as you put me in a hard spot making me decide. If i come with you, i can't because you have the others, and i Love**

you both, but i won't sign the papers, because after dad will be on his own". She then left, as that had been her first attempt to win me. It was strange, for the first time she spoke normal to me, no shouting, no threats, no Slaps, this was not a normal moment, for once she made me feel that this is what a good family was all about, calm talks, not pushing me to do things i hadn't want, though most of all she had 'Asked Me', to decide. The second time she returned must have been the fifth or sixth atempt, as she had caught me at home, but more likely waiting for me to return. She asked me how i was, and reminded me of how i was hardly ever home now. **"Please Paul"**, she started. **"I didn't come here to take you away from your father, but i tell you for your own good to come live with me and your brother and sisters".** I knew it, as this is one of the many reasons i hardly stayed home, i got upset with her and abruptly replied, **"I told you the first time, i did not ask for the divorce to happen, so don't put me in this position. Don't give me a hard time, your the one who decided to seperate the family, listening to Mariah. I don't want to speak about it again".** Then i closed the door again, leaving on my bike, making sure mother left the neighbourhood, then i returned home.

Mother caught me at home for the third time. i hadn't allowed her the chance to ask me again, as i answered before she could say anything, She then become cross with me, calling me stubborn, and a loser like my father. **"You don't know, your not old enough to know what you are doing, don't return to me when he destroys your life, how can you betray your mother, i nearly died for you at birth, and this is how you treat me".** she attempting the guilty trick as Mariah would with them. But it didn't work with me as it all came to an end, though for me, the fact of the matter had been, my mind was made up, as i was 'Happy to be Free'. All i desired most, was to explore the world that had been kept away from me all my life. I often visioned myself on my Bicycle, riding free, without anybody in mind, **"Just let me be Free, i have alot of catching up in life"**, give me my space, because this is all i need.

Folks, i know that most children live most of their Lives, 'Loving' their parents understanding over the years of this continous bond - **"Family"**.

Either it being a Happy, or otherwise, i guess the Future can't be any worse, as now i am in Full control, thanking my journey, to being where i am today, with the knowledge, and Experience, even better Late than Never, i'm on a mission as well as others would be, with that Goal towards Happiness as planned, i had been at 15 of age, when my dreams then, are my dreams now, as i am Persistant, i Shant give up..

I had been deeply scarred, and although i seemed normal to most people, it had always been a struggle, when 'Freedom' is all that i seek.

The next 20 years of my life had been a journey never expected, The outcome of setbacks due to Psychological conflicts remaining my enemy towards my future,

Life goes on...

To Be Continued.....